LLC & Taxes

Explained for Beginners

The Ultimate Step-By-Step Guide to Starting a Business,
Filing Taxes Correctly, Maximizing Deductions &
Staying IRS-Compliant

Pantheon Space Academy

Pantheon Space Academy

Printed Worldwide
First Printing 2025
First Edition 2025

10 9 8 7 6 5 4 3 2 1

Interior Book Design by Walt's Book Design
www.waltsbookdesign.com

Disclaimer Notice:

Please note the information contained within this document is for educational and entertainment purposes only. All efforts have been executed to present accurate, up-to-date, reliable, and complete information. No warranties of any kind are declared or implied. Readers acknowledge that the author does not render legal, financial, medical, or professional advice. The content within this book has been derived from various sources. Please consult a licensed professional before attempting any techniques outlined in this book.

By reading this document, the reader agrees that under no circumstances is the author responsible for any direct or indirect losses incurred due to the use of the information contained within this document, including, but not limited to, errors, omissions, or inaccuracies.

LLC & Taxes

Explained for Beginners

Table of Contents

Let's be real…

No one starts a business just to drown in paperwork and IRS regulations. You started an LLC to protect your assets, build a side hustle, or create financial freedom. The U.S. tax code is over 7,000 pages, and if you count regulations and interpretations, it stretches beyond 70,000 pages. Who has time for that?

But, the tax questions kept piling up.

- "Wait, when do I need to file taxes?"

- "Can I write off my laptop? What is classified as a home office?"

- "What's an S-Corp, and should I have one?"

- "How do I pay myself from my LLC, and what taxes do I owe?"

- "What deductions am I missing that could save me thousands?"

Meet **Alex**– a new LLC owner, just like you. Alex was **excited to start their business**—finally free from the 9-to-5, chasing a dream. But as soon as tax season hit, the stress became overwhelming. **IRS jargon, confusing forms, and the fear of costly mistakes** made it hard to focus on what really mattered—**running the business.**

This guide gives you exactly what you need—clear, practical strategies to help you save money, stay compliant, and grow your business without hiring an accountant or losing sleep. Starting a company is exciting, and it should feel that way! This book helps you spend less time stressed and more time doing what you love—while keeping more of your money.

Who is this book for:

- **Small Business Owners** looking for clear, actionable tax strategies to minimize tax liability legally and keep more of their hard-earned money.

- **Existing LLC Owners** who want to avoid IRS red flags, maximize deductions, and ensure tax compliance.

- **Freelancers & Independent Contractors** who want to know if forming an LLC is the right move for their business and how it will affect their taxes.

- **Side Hustlers & Online Business Owners** seeking guidance on structuring their business properly for tax efficiency.

- **Aspiring Entrepreneurs** who are considering forming an LLC and want to understand the tax benefits and obligations before starting.

No matter where you are in your business journey, this book will provide practical insights, step-by-step guidance, and real-world strategies to help you navigate LLC taxes. You'll learn how to file correctly, avoid common mistakes, and take advantage of tax-saving opportunities that many business owners overlook.

Exclusive Bonuses: Free Downloads to Help You Succeed

Managing your LLC's taxes involves more than just reading a book—it requires real tools to apply what you've learned. That's why your book purchase includes **free downloadable resources** to make tax management easier for you. These practical tools will help you **start, track, and scale** your LLC efficiently.

Essential IRS & LLC Forms

✔ **Form W-9** – Request for Taxpayer Identification Number (Useful for freelancers & contractors)

✔ **Form 1065** – Partnership Return (For multi-member LLCs)

✔ **Form 8832** – Entity Classification Election (If LLCs elect to be taxed as a corporation)

✔ **Schedule C (Form 1040)** – Business Profit/Loss Report (For single-member LLCs)

✔ **IRS Estimated Tax Payment Vouchers** – (For quarterly tax payments)

Business Checklists

✔ **LLC Startup Checklist** – Everything needed to form an LLC

✔ **LLC Tax Filing Checklist** – Step-by-step tax prep & filing

✔ **Deduction Maximization Checklist** – Common deductions LLC owners can take

✔ **Quarterly & Year-End Tax Checklist** – To help keep taxes on track

Financial Tools & Spreadsheets

✔ **Profit & Loss Statement** – Track revenue, expenses & net income

✔ **Expense Tracker Spreadsheet** – Organize business spending for tax deductions

Optional Business Documents

✔ **LLC Operating Agreement Template** – Customize your LLC's legal structure

✔ **Independent Contractor Agreement** – For hiring freelancers or contractors

Expertly Curated FAQ Section

✔ Covers **common tax, filing, and LLC business questions** with direct answers

Success Roadmap

✔ **LLC Success Roadmap PDF** – A **friendly, easy-to-follow timeline** of what to do from start to scaling

How to Access Your Free Downloads:

All of these resources are available in one convenient location. Get instant access to all your bonus resources! Visit **https://www.pantheonspace.com/LLC** or scan the QR code now.

If you have any trouble accessing the bonus files, please email support@pantheonspace.com

Introduction

Effective tax strategies improve your financial outlook as a small business owner in a radical way. Maybe you've felt the tension of tax season creeping up or unsure if you're handling everything just right. It happens to all of us. Small business owners, entrepreneurs, freelancers, and students getting into the world of taxation often face these challenges, taxes can be overwhelming and feel like an obstacle rather than an opportunity, but what if they could help you build your dream rather than hold it back?

Let me tell you the story of a hardworking entrepreneur, Sarah, who started a cozy little bakery nestled in her neighborhood. In 2019, she left her decade-long career as a pastry chef to open Honeycomb Bakery, a 900-square-foot storefront in a busy town center. Within eighteen months, her signature cardamom morning buns and sourdough croissants had earned a loyal local following. Her revenue had climbed to $428,000, and she'd grown from two employees to seven. However, in March 2021, she learned about a critical oversight in her business planning: she hadn't properly structured her quarterly estimated tax payment for her LLC. When tax season arrived, she faced an unexpected $47,000 tax bill, which turned out to be funds she'd already earmarked for a second location. Now, that brought consequences, of course. She had to postpone hiring two new bakers and delay purchasing a $38,000 commercial oven that would have doubled her production capacity. This experience is a common pitfall with LLCs and taxes, especially among first-time business owners who underestimate the complexity of LLC tax obligations and their impact on growth plans.

This book is a wake-up call for anyone starting or operating a small business. Sarah's experience explains why understanding the intricacies of LLC taxation is important—not just to fulfill legal requirements but to thrive and grow. With the right strategies, what seems like an intimidating tax code could instead become a roadmap to reinvesting in your passion and fortifying your future. This advice is not all about compliance but also about empowerment, turning uncertainty into clarity, and fear into control.

For small business owners and entrepreneurs, understanding LLC taxation means opportunities for greater financial security. The IRS might seem like a formidable giant at first glance, but going through its complexities with knowledge and strategy can yield dividends that go far beyond saving money—think growth, peace of mind, and freedom to focus on what truly matters: your business aspirations. As we go through various strategies and insights, you'll see how others have used them to comply with regulations and to their advantage while maximizing profitability and ensuring their ventures are sustainable and successful.

Entrepreneurs, startups, and self-employed individuals share a common goal—confidently walking the complex tax terrain. It can be daunting and full of complex forms, deadlines, and obscure terms, but this is what we will tackle in this book. We're going to demystify these complexities, providing clear, actionable advice that will lead you step by step toward mastering LLC tax responsibilities. If you're going to start your own company or are already managing daily operations, this guide will match your circumstances and needs. You'll learn every detail, from foundational tax principles to quick ways to reduce tax burdens.

If you're a student dreaming of becoming a tax consultant or simply wishing to grasp small business financial management, you've picked up the right book. We'll address real-world scenarios and practical examples, helping you acquire the expertise needed to understand this field. When walking through the essentials of LLC taxation, you'll build a foundation for advising others—or perhaps even launching your own venture with foresight and savvy.

Looking ahead, we'll get into structured topics to equip and empower you. From essential bookkeeping practices and LLC-specific deductions to the importance of planning and the intricacies of quarterly taxes, each chapter unfolds valuable insights and practical advice. You'll understand strategies used by seasoned entrepreneurs to reduce tax stress and turn liabilities into opportunities for growth. These chapters will show you clear paths to success and sustainability.

What you'll learn in these pages covers far more than figures and forms. This book is a tool for transformation—a blueprint for reassessing your approach, learning about business strategies, and understanding and embracing a mindset that sees challenges as chances to excel. Each tool and insight offers solutions that support your goals. This knowledge will lead to greater financial freedom and business success.

After reading this book, the once overwhelming world of taxes will seem less intimidating and more integral to your business journey, giving you the power to make informed decisions with the knowledge and confidence to back them up. So let's get started together—you, me, and a wealth of knowledge waiting to unfold, all geared toward helping you unlock the full potential of your business dreams.

Chapter 1: Introduction to LLC Taxation

Knowing LLC taxation is essential for anyone managing or starting the process of LLC formation. With its blend of benefits, an LLC combines operational flexibility with relevant liability protection, and with that mixture, it presents a compelling choice for many business owners. However, going through the taxation world can seem like a lot, filled with terms and regulations that might feel like a whole new language. Let's demystify the basics of LLC taxation in simple terms. You'll get a glimpse into why grasping these fundamentals matters so much when you're protecting your personal assets or optimizing your business's financial health.

You'll learn about key aspects of LLC taxation without the overwhelming jargon, understand how LLCs offer tax advantages such as pass-through taxation (which helps you avoid the double taxation seen in corporations), and we'll also dig into the flexibility you have when it comes to choosing how your LLC is taxed—regardless of being a sole proprietorship, partnership, S corporation, or C corporation—and why this decision is so important.

Definition and Structure of an LLC

Anyone considering this business structure must understand what an LLC is and how it operates. An LLC offers distinct advantages, primarily in protecting personal assets from the business's liabilities. This feature reduces personal financial risk, which is attractive to many entrepreneurs and small business owners. When you set up an LLC, you can be sure that your personal property, such as homes or savings, remains secure if the business incurs debts or faces legal challenges.

Formation Process

Setting up an LLC needs some straightforward steps, starting with filing articles of organization with the state where the business will operate. These steps are clear and easy to follow. Filing these articles creates the LLC as a separate legal entity, so you can start running your business. The simplicity of forming an LLC is one of its appealing features, drawing in those who wish to establish a business without dealing with complex legal requirements.

What makes an LLC special is its flexibility in management and membership. Unlike corporations that often need a board of directors and a set governance structure, you can structure your LLC how you want. An LLC can have either single-member or multi-member participation. This design means you can start alone or join forces with others, creating diverse management styles and operational practices. Decision-making is usually more agile in a single-member LLC, whereas multi-member configurations can bring in varied expertise and shared responsibilities. Let's look at the concrete steps:

Step 1: Choose your business name and check availability:

Before filing any paperwork, you must choose a unique business name that complies with your state's requirements. Your LLC name must:

- end with a proper designator (LLC, L.L.C., or Limited Liability Company).

- be distinguishable from other registered businesses in your state.

- avoid restricted words that might require additional licenses.

- not violate any trademarks.

Step 2: Designate a registered agent:

Every LLC must have a registered agent. This agent is someone or a company authorized to receive legal documents on behalf of your business. This agent must:

- maintain a physical address (not a P.O. box) in the state of registration.

- be available during regular business hours.

- be at least 18 years old if an individual.

- agree to accept legal documents on behalf of the LLC.

Step 3: File articles of organization

This document formally establishes your LLC with the state. The articles usually require:

- your LLC's name and principal business address.

- your registered agent's information.

- the LLC's purpose and duration.

- management structure (member-managed or manager-managed).

- names and addresses of founding members.

- filing fees, which vary by state ($50 to $500).

Step 4: Create an operating agreement

This form might not be required in every state, but an operating agreement is important for:

- defining ownership percentages and voting rights.

- establishing management structure and roles.

- outlining profit and loss distribution.

- setting procedures for member changes.

- determining dissolution processes.

Step 5: Obtain required permits and licenses

Once your LLC is officially formed, the next step is to secure the necessary permits and licenses to operate legally is the next step. Depending on your industry and location, you may need to:

- apply for an EIN from the IRS.

- secure state-specific business licenses.

- obtain industry-specific permits.

- register for state tax accounts.

Ownership Flexibility

Different types of owners can join LLCs. Unlike sole proprietorships or partnerships, which usually only allow individual ownership, many different entities can own an LLC. Depending on state laws, this includes individuals, other LLCs, corporations, or even foreign investors. This variety helps create strategic partnerships and innovative collaborations. As an example, an LLC could include stakeholders from different industries, using each owner's strengths and networks.

An LLC blends elements of corporations and partnerships, allowing business owners to customize operations. This flexible structure can better support your specific needs. Its adaptability makes it easier to scale, pivot, or restructure as your business evolves. It also fosters creative problem-solving and growth strategies, helping you stay competitive in a dynamic market.

LLCs offer tax advantages by passing profits to owners without corporate tax. This pass-through taxation means that income is reported on the members' personal tax returns, reducing the overall tax burden. Members can enjoy the benefits of owning a business without the complexity and expense of double taxation that affects corporations. However, you need to know your responsibilities regarding self-employment taxes and prepare accordingly.

Although LLCs provide a shield against business liabilities, members should be aware of scenarios where personal liability might arise. Personal guarantees and fraudulent mixing of personal and business can break your liability protection. So, maintaining clear boundaries between personal and business dealings is necessary. Members should also learn about their fiduciary duties and follow best practices to uphold the integrity of the LLC structure.

Remember that while LLCs generally offer continuity of existence similar to corporations, you need to follow certain rules to keep it running. One way to do this is to draft a well-structured operating agreement that includes procedures for transferring ownership or passing on membership interests, creating a seamless business transition when necessary. This document becomes an internal guideline for operations and member interactions, helping to resolve potential disputes and preserving the LLC's long-term success.

Knowing the benefits and limitations of an LLC is important for small business owners and startups planning growth within a flexible framework. When you understand the unique combination of liability protection, managerial freedom, and tax advantages, you can make informed decisions about structuring your ventures. You can also use the LLC's inherent versatility for specific business models and industry demands to create sustained success.

Overview of Tax Benefits for LLCs

When it comes to business structures, LLCs give you a unique set of tax advantages that can be especially appealing to small business owners. Knowing these benefits is relevant for anyone considering this structure for their enterprise.

Pass-Through Taxation

Unlike corporations, where profits are taxed at both the corporate level and again at the individual level when distributed as dividends, LLCs benefit from a feature known as "pass-through" taxation. This means that the profits of the LLC are reported on the owners' personal tax returns, thus avoiding the dreaded double taxation commonly associated with corporations. In other words, this simplifies the overall taxation process and, at the same time, makes it more efficient for business owners. Let's look at an example. Say that your LLC makes $100,000 in profit this year. Instead of the business paying taxes and then you also paying taxes when you take it as income (by the way, this is what happens with corporations), that $100,000 simply "passes through" to your personal tax return. This process means that you only pay tax once, and in this case, at your individual tax rate. This tax hack can save a lot of money because you're not taxed twice.

The simplicity of pass-through taxation can benefit small business owners. When profits flow to the owners without the intermediary corporate-level tax, LLC owners can better manage their finances. This structure makes it easier to plan for taxes since you focus on your personal tax liability rather than handling the complexities of corporate taxes. Many entrepreneurs, especially those starting their businesses, find this more straightforward approach a major advantage. Also, managing your business taxes can be less stressful, and knowing that your earnings will not be taxed twice can give you peace of mind. Instead of worrying about manipulating numbers to fit a corporate tax structure, you can focus on growing your business and using profits for investment or personal needs without the burden of extra tax calculations. This efficiency in taxation can help you make smarter financial decisions.

LLC owners should keep accurate records throughout the year to correctly manage the personal tax implications. Be diligent. Documenting income and expenses will make the tax filing process smoother, and an organized method will help you report the right amount on your tax return. You should consult with a professional tax advisor to clarify any specific concerns or details about your situation.

They can provide valuable insights into maximizing your deductions and minimizing your taxable income, which can be particularly helpful in a pass-through taxation framework. Due to the flexibility of LLCs allowing for various distribution options, owners can choose how to distribute profits among themselves, which can further optimize tax outcomes. When one owner has a lower tax bracket, you may allocate more profits to that individual. This tax hack can help reduce the owners' overall tax burden. You can reinvest profits back into the business for growth instead of taking distributions, allowing for the potential for compound growth without immediate tax consequences.

Pass-through taxation also affects how business partners define their contributions within the LLC. Because profits and losses are reported on individual tax returns, each member's financial situation can influence decision-making. This factor can lead to discussions about how much profit each partner should receive based on their work in the business or their financial needs. Open communication matters; all partners must understand how distributions will occur and how they impact their taxes. If you're thinking about starting an LLC, pass-through taxation can be a compelling reason to choose this structure over a corporation. It simplifies the tax process and helps you handle income tax as an individual, reducing concerns about corporate tax compliance. This approach lets your business operate efficiently while keeping tax obligations in check.

Deductions and Write-Offs

LLCs have the flexibility to deduct legitimate business expenses. This capacity increases financial management within the business and offers substantial tax savings. When you are able to track and claim these expenses, you can reduce your taxable income, which in turn lowers the amount of taxes you owe. Consider an LLC owner who consistently incurs costs such as travel, office supplies, or employee salaries. All these can be deducted when calculating the profit subject to tax, which means that the LLC's tax burden could be significantly minimized. For many entrepreneurs, this deduction potential is pivotal in maintaining healthy cash flow and reinvesting back into the business.

Flexible Tax Classification

One other standout feature of an LLC is its flexible tax classification options. LLCs can choose to be taxed in different ways, depending on what aligns best with their financial goals. They have the option to choose a partnership, S corporation, or C corporation tax setup. This flexibility lets business owners like you strategically plan your taxes based on your specific circumstances. Say that an LLC that chooses to be taxed as an S corporation can take advantage of lower self-employment taxes through salary and distribution methodologies. This strategic planning capability can lead to significant savings and a reduced tax liability.

Another practical example is an LLC owner opting to be taxed as an S corporation. This type lets them pay themselves a reasonable salary, accounting for employment taxes, while treating the remaining income as a distribution that isn't subject to self-employment taxes. This tactic alleviates some of the financial burdens associated with self-employment taxes and, at the same time, leverages provisions like the Qualified Business Income deduction, which allows eligible business owners to exclude up to 20% of their business income from taxes. Such tax strategies underline how important it is for LLC owners to evaluate their status regularly and make tax elections that align with their current needs and future objectives (Coombes, 2023).

The ability for owners to pick their tax structure doesn't end there. Choosing a C corporation setup isn't always popular due to high corporate tax rates, yet it still holds a certain appeal for businesses planning for growth that requires reinvestment, without immediate concern for distributions to members. The relatively recent changes in tax legislation have made certain deductions and credits more accessible, potentially altering tax liabilities in favor of the business.

LLCs offer a combination of operational simplicity, owner protection, and tax flexibility, making them an attractive choice for a wide range of businesses. However, it is important to consult with tax professionals or legal advisors to understand the complexities of each available tax structure fully. Each business's situation is unique, and understanding how different tax setups can affect your long-term financial strategy is invaluable.

Importance of Tax Compliance

Now, on to managing an LLC. Understanding and adhering to tax regulations is not only a legal requirement but also essential for long-term business success. Failing to comply can lead to audits, fines, and legal risks—jeopardizing your LLC's good standing. That's why staying compliant is a must for protecting your business and ensuring smooth operations.

Legal Consequences

First, consider the serious consequences of neglecting tax compliance. Audits by the Internal Revenue Service (IRS) can be both time-consuming and costly. They often arise from discrepancies in tax filings, missed deadlines, or incomplete record-keeping. Should the IRS find wrongdoing, the penalties can include substantial fines. Such financial burdens can strain or even cripple small businesses, highlighting the importance of prioritizing tax compliance from the outset.

Maintaining Good Standing

Also, keeping up with compliance allows your LLC to retain its legal status. An LLC provides liability protection to its owners, shielding personal assets from business liabilities. However, this protective feature may be compromised if your LLC falls out of compliance. Say, for example, that you fail to file necessary annual reports or pay franchise taxes as required by state law. This could lead to the administrative dissolution of the LLC. This scenario would strip away the liability protections and potentially expose members' personal assets to business claims. So, if you stay compliant, you ensure continuity and operational stability, allowing your business to operate smoothly and without unnecessary legal hurdles.

Staying Informed

Tax laws change frequently. So, learning about these changes helps you stay compliant and avoid unexpected legal issues. With legislation often evolving at both federal and state levels, staying updated may be overwhelming, but it's essential nonetheless. Reading updates from tax authorities or consulting with a tax professional can help you learn about new obligations and adjust your practices as needed.

Another important aspect of compliance is its direct impact on a business's credibility and reputation. Consistently meeting regulatory requirements reflects responsible management and promotes trust with clients, partners, and investors. Businesses known for maintaining high ethical standards and transparency are more likely to attract favorable partnerships and investment opportunities. On the other hand, a history marred with compliance issues can deter potential collaborators and customers, stalling growth prospects.

Setting up solid internal processes is beneficial for effectively managing compliance. These would involve regular audits of financial records, timely submission of all relevant documents, and ongoing education about applicable laws. Implementing a system to track deadlines and documentation requirements helps prevent oversights. At the same time, using document templates for standard procedures—such as operating agreements and meeting minutes—can simplify the internal process, making compliance less cumbersome.

Having a registered agent to receive official correspondence and reminders about filing requirements is another practical measure to streamline compliance efforts. This way, you know that your LLC doesn't miss critical communication from government bodies and helps to avert non-compliance issues.

Consistent compliance protects against fines and legal troubles and positions a business favorably during important moments like securing financing or negotiating a sale. Lenders and investors often scrutinize a company's compliance history as part of their due diligence process. A track record of adherence to regulations can improve an LLC's appeal, yielding more favorable terms and conditions in financial engagements.

For those new to LLC management or considering forming one, using resources for small businesses can make learning easier. Workshops, seminars, and online courses focused on understanding tax obligations can help entrepreneurs with the knowledge necessary to uphold compliance without undue stress.

In the end, adding these practices into daily operations secures your business legally and strategically positions it for long-term sustainability. By emphasizing the necessity of staying compliant, you can avoid the pitfalls associated with non-compliance, maintain your good standing, and promote a solid foundation that supports growth and resilience.

Practical Strategies

Beyond general knowledge, the book also discusses practical strategies customized to your needs. We'll guide you through methods for tracking expenses and maximizing deductions, which are important for minimizing your taxable income. For example, keeping organized records and categorizing transactions correctly simplifies tax reporting and helps identify deductible expenses. The importance of separating personal and business finances will be highlighted; it's a simple yet effective practice that ensures you're legally protected and have transparent financial management.

Simplifying tax regulations by using relatable examples and scenarios helps ground theoretical knowledge in real-world applications. Imagine you're a self-employed individual eager to optimize your tax filings. When you apply the guidelines shared in this book, such as leveraging accounting software for automation and expense tracking, you'll see improvements in efficiency and accuracy. These tools are relevant and offer accessibility while further streamlining data entry tasks.

Navigating Complexity

Throughout this journey, we'll highlight the value of foundational understanding in making informed financial decisions. Consider a startup founder debating whether to handle accounting in-house or outsource it. With a solid grasp of LLC taxation principles, you'll better examine the complexity of your financial transactions and the resources available, so choose the best option for your business.

Again, staying updated on changing tax laws is critical to maintaining compliance. This book emphasizes the importance of continuous learning opportunities offered by software providers and professional organizations like the American Institute of Certified Public Accountants (AICPA). Adapting technology and ongoing education are essential for businesses that aim to stay compliant with evolving regulations.

As your guide, this book makes sure you remain well-informed and prepared to effectively handle whatever challenges the tax landscape presents. Our mission is to give you the knowledge that goes beyond compliance and becomes a tool for growth—enabling you to make strategic decisions that benefit your financial health and business stability.

Final Insights

Now that you understand the basics of LLC taxation, you can see why these concepts matter for anyone involved with this type of business structure. We covered everything from the definition and setup of an LLC to its standout feature of pass-through taxation, which means profits are directly reported on the owners' personal tax returns. This step-by-step guide eases the tax process and prevents double taxation, making financial life easier for small business owners and entrepreneurs alike. You also learned about the flexibility in ownership and management styles, showing that LLCs work how you want, whether you're going solo or teaming up with others.

Using tax benefits an LLC offers, like deducting legitimate business expenses, can make a huge difference to your bottom line. Being able to choose how your LLC is taxed—whether as a partnership, S corporation, or C corporation—gives you the kind of control over your finances that can lead to smarter, more strategic decision-making. In the following chapter, we will get into how different LLC tax classifications work and help you pick the one that fits your business goals.

Chapter 2: LLC Tax Classifications Explained

Understanding LLC tax classifications can directly affect how your business is taxed and managed. LLCs have multiple options in choosing a tax classification that matches your business best, including options as a sole proprietorship, partnership, or corporation, but choosing the right tax setup isn't just about picking one that seems easiest or most familiar; it's about aligning with your business goals and understanding the ins and outs of each option. Each decision carries its own set of pros and cons, affecting everything from your personal liability to the types of taxes you'll need to pay.

This chapter covers the specifics of the different tax classifications available for LLCs. The explanations begin with how sole proprietorship taxation works and why it might be an attractive choice for single-member LLCs. You'll also learn about the partnership approach, offering insights into how sharing tax responsibilities can benefit multi-member LLCs.

Sole Proprietorship Taxation

LLCs are incredibly flexible when it comes to taxation. One of the most straightforward and common tax classifications is treating an LLC as a sole proprietorship. This choice is appealing for single-member LLCs as it streamlines the process while offering specific financial benefits. Let's examine how this works and what it means for individual tax liability.

Tax Filing Process

When an LLC opts to be taxed as a sole proprietorship, it simplifies the tax filing process. Instead of having to file a separate business tax return, the income from the LLC is reported directly on the owner's personal tax return using Schedule C. This type of reporting makes it easier for single-member LLC owners to handle their taxes without the need for additional paperwork or complex filings. It allows you to present profit or loss from the business in their annual tax filings (*LLC Filing as a Corporation or Partnership*, 2024).

Self-Employment Taxes

As you might have guessed, with these advantages come responsibilities regarding self-employment taxes. As an owner of a single-member LLC taxed as a sole proprietorship, you are responsible for paying self-employment tax. This payment includes the employer and employee portions of Social Security and Medicare taxes, which can take up a significant chunk of your earnings. For many small business owners and entrepreneurs, planning ahead by setting aside funds throughout the year to meet these obligations is critical. Also, you have to know about potential deductions, as these can lower your tax liability. Deductions such as home office expenses, travel, supplies, and utilities can help soften the blow of self-employment taxes (Fontinelle, 2024).

Advantages and Disadvantages

Simplicity is undoubtedly one of the main benefits of being taxed as a sole proprietorship. It cuts down on administrative tasks and provides clarity in terms of personal finances since everything is consolidated under one tax return. This simplicity does come with a trade-off, however: personal liability. Unlike other tax classifications that might offer more protection, choosing this route means that the owner is personally liable for any debts or legal actions taken against the business. This exposure is relevant when assessing whether to choose this classification, especially if your business carries substantial risk or debt.

There's also another financial angle to consider in specific scenarios. If your LLC operates in an industry where liabilities are high, it might not be advisable to remain taxed as a sole proprietorship. In such cases, the potential risks could outweigh the benefits of a simplified tax process, so evaluating the nature of your business and the extent of any personal liabilities is essential before deciding on this tax approach.

Consider the financial cushion you have. If your business has substantial debt or needs to finance growth, then the personal liability aspect becomes even more critical. Suppose you're unsure whether you can manage the risks associated with personal liability. In that case, you should explore other business structures that offer more protection, such as forming an LLC or a corporation. These options can shield your personal assets from business liabilities. While they might need more complex tax filings and administrative work, the added protection can be worth it in high-risk scenarios. As you weigh all these factors, performing a self-assessment of your business can be beneficial. Ask yourself questions like, "What industry do I operate in?" "What are the potential risks associated with my business?" "How much debt do I currently have?" After answering these questions, you can determine the possible impacts of your tax classification. This evaluation will help you balance the ease of a sole proprietorship with the financial risks. A methodical review of your business's needs will guide you in making the best decision for your situation.

Also, consider the growth trajectory of your business. If you plan to expand your operations, consider switching your tax classification. As a sole proprietor, attracting investors or partners can be challenging. Forming an LLC or corporation might be better if you want to bring in partners or seek investment capital. These business structures offer a more appealing picture to potential investors, as they show a separation between personal and business finances. They also provide more credibility and transparency to your business operations, which can be important as you look to grow.

In summary, while the advantages of being taxed as a sole proprietorship are clear, particularly regarding simplicity and ease of tax filing, the disadvantages, especially concerning personal liability, are equally significant. The risks of running your business as a sole proprietorship should be carefully weighed against the convenience it offers. Understanding your business's nature, financial stability, and growth potential can help you make a more informed decision. Each business is unique, and what works for one may not work for another. Taking the time to evaluate these factors can lead to a more secure financial path in the long run.

Case Study

To better understand how sole proprietorship taxation looks in practice, let's break it down with an example. Say that you run a small graphic design business as a single-member LLC. Over the course of the year, your company earns $50,000 in revenue. After deducting related expenses such as software subscriptions, hardware costs, and marketing fees totaling $15,000, you're left with a net income of $35,000. When tax season rolls around, you'll report this income on Schedule C, attached to your Form 1040.

From there, you'll calculate your self-employment taxes based on this $35,000 net income. At approximately 15.3%, these taxes would amount to around $5,355. However, don't forget about those deductions! If eligible, they can reduce your overall taxable income, helping to lower the final tax bill owed. Accurate record-keeping is crucial to ensuring you claim every deduction available. Proper documentation throughout the year can substantially reduce your self-employment taxes, making them more manageable.

Using real numbers and walking through the tax process for a sole proprietorship, it's quite clear how this classification plays out for a single-member LLC owner. Despite the ease offered by sole proprietorship status, weighing the simplicity against potential personal liabilities helps determine if it's right for everyone. For some, the reduced complexity in tax preparation and the direct integration with personal income tax returns make this an appealing choice. However, always keep the broader financial and legal context within which your business operates in mind.

Partnership Taxation

Having a good grasp of LLC tax responsibilities and opportunities is essential for any small business owner. An increasingly popular option among LLC owners is electing partnership taxation, which allows for flexible distribution of tax responsibilities based on what best suits the business's needs.

Formation of Partnership

In the context of business structures, forming partnerships within an LLC can give you significant flexibility, especially when it comes to ownership arrangements. A multi-member LLC will usually default to being taxed as a partnership unless another classification is elected, such as corporation status through Form 8832 (*LLC Filing as a Corporation or Partnership*, 2024). However, when you maintain a partnership structure, members have the benefit of customizing their profit-sharing based on their contributions or agreements made within the LLC. However, with this flexibility come certain compliance requirements. The LLC must adhere to various federal and state regulations, making sure all legal standards are met and agreements between partners are clearly documented.

Tax Returns for Partnerships

When an LLC elects partnership taxation, it needs a clear understanding of specific IRS forms such as Form 1065 and Schedule K-1. Form 1065 is the U.S. Return of Partnership Income, where the LLC reports its total income, deductions, and credits to the IRS. Each partner then receives a K-1 form detailing their share of the partnership's income, which they report on their personal tax returns. It's important for LLCs opting for partnership taxation to keep meticulous records. To do this, you must track all financial transactions and maintain transparency among partners regarding income, expenses, and all related allocations (*Beneficial Ownership Information*, n.d.).

Pros and Cons

A main aspect of partnership taxation is the shared responsibility among members. With shared tax responsibilities, each member is liable for their proportionate share of the tax burden based on the partnership agreement. While this can be beneficial, allowing each partner to manage their tax liabilities individually, it also needs thorough planning so there's a fair distribution of both profits and losses. In this circumstance, members should consider establishing clear guidelines on how profits will be distributed to avoid potential disputes.

Keep in mind that this kind of setup can lead to increased complexity in tax filings. Partnerships demand more communication and detailed financial reporting compared to more straightforward structures like sole proprietorships. To mitigate these complexities, LLCs should invest time in creating well-crafted operating agreements and use accounting software for precise record-keeping (*LLC Filing as a Corporation or Partnership*, 2024).

To get the most out of partnership taxation, you need to use practical strategies like effective profit-sharing agreements. These agreements define how profits are split and should also establish expectations for every member's financial contributions and obligations. These types of clear agreements can reduce misunderstandings and support smoother operations. Also, LLCs can capitalize on potential deductions across partners by developing comprehensive tax plans. For example, you can claim expenses such as office supplies, depreciation, and other ordinary business expenses to lower taxable income.

You should also promote open communication about financial responsibilities, which is very important for a successful partnership. Regular meetings, transparent discussions, and accurate documentation allow all members to align with the LLC's financial strategies and goals. When everybody understands their role and the business's financial health, it promotes trust and long-term cooperation among partners.

Corporation Taxation

The decision to have your LLC taxed as a corporation is a significant step that requires many different things to be considered. The most important thing in this process is Form 8832, which allows an LLC to elect for corporate tax treatment. This election can be strategic for businesses looking to benefit from certain aspects of corporate taxation. When you file, Form 8832 matters. New LLCs should consider filing as a corporation early on to take advantage of potential tax savings, while established businesses often benefit from it if their operations grow in size or scope.

Tax Election Process

Let's now look at how one might make this election. An LLC may be taxed as a corporation to reduce the burden of self-employment taxes, particularly if there are sizable profits. Corporations may offer attractive options for reinvestment and growth due to their ability to retain earnings internally. It's imperative to remember that choosing the incorrect tax status can result in serious consequences, so consulting with a tax professional before making any decisions is advised.

Double Taxation Explained

A key consideration when an LLC elects to be taxed as a corporation is double taxation—a system in which corporate profits are taxed at the entity level. Then, dividends paid to shareholders are taxed again at the individual level. This dual-layer taxation can significantly reduce your business's net income, making it a meaningful factor in tax planning.

For example, if a corporation makes $100,000 in profit, this amount will initially be taxed. If the remaining profit, after taxes, is distributed as dividends to shareholders, those dividends are also subject to taxes. However, there are strategies to mitigate these effects. Businesses often focus on reinvesting profits back into the company or choosing compensation methods like bonuses, which can lower taxable dividends.

Advantages and Disadvantages

Before choosing corporate taxation, consider the pros and cons. One of the primary advantages of opting for corporate tax treatment is the limited liability protection it offers. This insulates personal assets from business liabilities. It can be appealing for owners wary of putting personal finances at risk, and corporations might find it easier to raise capital, as investors often prefer investing in this familiar structure. There are, however, drawbacks to consider. Corporate compliance includes more complex regulatory requirements, which can lead to higher administrative costs.

Real-world examples illustrate these dynamics: Some tech startups opt for corporate classification early to prepare for future public offerings, while others remain pass-through entities to keep accounting simple and tax obligations minimal until growth demands otherwise.

However, there are notable drawbacks associated with corporate taxation. One significant downside is the complexity of corporate compliance. Businesses structured as corporations must follow regulations and legal requirements, which can be quite complicated. They must hold annual meetings, maintain detailed records, and file specific reports with government agencies. This can lead to increased administrative costs, as more staff or professional services may be needed to handle these responsibilities. A key factor for business owners is that corporate taxation might not always be the most cost-effective option. Depending on how much profit the business makes, the overall tax burden could be higher compared to pass-through taxation. Pass-through entities, such as partnerships or sole proprietorships, allow profits to be taxed only once at the owners' personal income tax rates. This strategy can lead to significant tax savings for some businesses, especially in their early stages when revenues are lower. So, the decision on whether to elect corporate taxation should also consider the business's current and projected financial performance.

Examples of this decision-making process can be quite informative. Some tech startups that expect rapid growth may opt for corporate classification early on, viewing it as a strategic move to position themselves for future investments or public offerings. This choice allows them to create the infrastructure necessary for scaling, regardless of current financial burdens. Many startups and small businesses prefer to remain as pass-through entities for as long as possible. They keep their accounting straightforward and focus on minimizing tax obligations. This simplicity allows them to reinvest profits back into the business without the additional complexity of corporate compliance.

Before choosing, business owners should carefully assess their unique circumstances. Analyzing the potential risks and rewards of corporate versus pass-through taxation can help clarify the best path forward. Consulting with a financial advisor or tax professional can provide valuable insights tailored to your situation, as they can help outline the tax implications of each structure and assist in developing a long-term business strategy that aligns with personal financial goals. Choosing between corporate taxation and other forms needs careful consideration of various factors. Understanding the limited liability protection, easier access to capital, and regulatory requirements is important. Weighing the potential tax benefits of pass-through entities may lead some to reconsider the corporate route. By examining these variables, business owners can make better decisions that support their current objectives while preparing for future success.

Strategic Considerations

Think carefully about your goals before making the shift toward corporate tax status. Working with a tax professional can give you specific insights into your business's circumstances. These experts will assess current and projected earnings, weigh the benefits of deferring income, and understand any state-specific nuances, such as varied deduction rules or local taxation impacts (*Beneficial Ownership Information*, n.d.). As your business grows, review your tax status to match with current operational needs. For instance, a small family-owned LLC might remain under default classification in its early years. As the business grows, switching to corporate status could align better with expansion plans.

Another strategy involves evaluating state-level tax implications. Some states allow deductions on federal taxes for LLCs taxed as C-corporations, which can potentially reduce the effective state income tax rate. Balancing these benefits against the added complexity of filing taxes at multiple levels—federal, state, and possibly local—requires careful planning.

Start this process by gathering your financial documents. This path includes balance sheets, income statements, and cash flow statements for the current year and previous years. Understanding your financial position will help you and your tax professional assess the potential benefits of changing your tax status. Create projections for future growth, which can clarify the advantages of switching to corporate status. Setting clear criteria for when to reassess your tax status can be helpful. When your revenue grows by a certain percentage or reaches a specific threshold, review your status. Setting these benchmarks helps you stay proactive and optimize your business's financial standing. Regular reviews of your eligibility for corporate status and understanding the rules can save your business significant tax liabilities.

Look at the structure of your business. If you operate as a sole proprietor, becoming a corporation could benefit you. A corporation limits personal liability, protecting your personal assets against business debts if your business faces lawsuits or financial difficulties. Filing as a corporation can improve credibility, and being an officially recognized corporate entity can expand your opportunities with suppliers and customers. They often view corporate businesses as more stable and trustworthy. This perception could lead to better contract terms or partnerships, supporting future growth.

Corporate status also affects employee benefits, which corporations can offer, attracting better talent. Health insurance, retirement plans, and stock options work better under corporate structures. If you want to expand your workforce, corporate tax status gives you more options for competitive benefits. Keep stakeholders informed during this transition. Be clear with employees, partners, and investors about tax status changes and their implications. Good communication helps create a smooth transition and keeps everyone aligned with business goals. Regular meetings and clear documentation help keep all parties informed and engaged.

Learn from others in your industry. Connect with other business owners for insights and strategies. Join local business groups or online forums to ask questions and share experiences. Learning how others handle similar decisions can guide your choices and inspire new ideas for growth. Changing to corporate tax status is a significant decision that requires a careful review of your goals, state requirements, and business structure. Professional advice, growth evaluation, and industry knowledge will help your business succeed long term.

Process of Electing Tax Status

Choosing tax classification for an LLC is important to understand the steps involved to make it manageable, especially for beginners.

Initial Considerations

Before choosing a tax status, you have to consider some initial factors that should count towards your decision. You need to evaluate the financial implications of each tax classification. For instance, as you know, choosing C-corporation status could lead to double taxation, whereas S-corporations avoid this issue but come with eligibility requirements like a limited number of shareholders. Think about how these classifications align with your business structure and goals. Do you want rapid growth, or is simplicity more valuable to your current operations? These considerations help build a foundation for a well-informed decision.

Filing Forms

Once you've weighed these factors, diving into the specifics of filing becomes necessary, and Form 8832 is the most important when picking your tax classification. You have to know how to fill this form accurately for a smooth election process.

You should begin by gathering required identifying information, such as your LLC's Employer Identification Number (EIN) and formation details. You have to provide complete and precise information to avoid processing delays. Then, pick the desired entity classification—either C corporation, S corporation, partnership, or disregarded entity—and ensure this choice aligns with your earlier considerations about business impacts (Poli, 2023).

Then, focus on the signature and attestation section. An authorized member must sign and date Form 8832, making sure all data is correctly entered before submission. Remember, for some tax classifications, additional forms may be required alongside Form 8832. Submission locations vary depending on your state, so consult the latest IRS guidelines to find out where to send the completed form. Timeliness is relevant here; the election generally takes effect 75 days after filing. Filing electronically can expedite the process if you're looking for quicker confirmation.

Post-Election Duties

After deciding and filing the necessary paperwork, there are post-election duties to consider. This strategy will depend on your chosen classification, and with this, different responsibilities arise. Once again, you have to regularly perform reviews. Tax laws and business circumstances change, and what's beneficial today might not be suitable tomorrow. Work with partners or advisors to stay on top of any necessary adjustments. Form 8832 classifications usually hold for at least five years, so consistent monitoring is important to make sure there is continued alignment between your business needs and tax obligations (Poli, 2023).

Examples and Case Studies

Imagine a scenario where a small business owner, Joanna, wants her LLC to be taxed as an S corporation. She begins by determining the financial impacts, considering her business's current financial health and future growth trajectories. This assessment helps her decide that avoiding double taxation outweighs the downsides of shareholder limitation. Joanna carefully fills out Form 8832, making sure she checks the box for S-corp status and verifies her EIN twice. She then signs the form, confirming her decision with her business advisor before submitting it to the appropriate IRS center within the allotted time frame.

Throughout this process, Joanna regularly interacted with her partners to keep everyone informed and aligned. She emphasized the importance of partner communication after the election. Her approach ensured no compliance issues arose, reinforcing that careful follow-up is as important as the initial election itself.

Let's look at another example. Alex is a tech startup founder who developed an AI-powered project management platform. Initially, operating as a single-member LLC, he began to explore the possibility of being taxed as a partnership. He initially disregarded this entity because he's the sole owner, handling everything from product development to client acquisition. However, Alex evaluated his plans to bring in two potential co-founders. He anticipated shared management responsibilities across product development, market expansion, and operational decisions, and sought the simplicity in tax filings that would work with this growth. Because of this, Alex completed Form 8832, opting for a partnership classification. He learned that meticulous record-keeping through Form 1065 will soon become part of his routine, needing detailed documentation of capital contributions. Yet, he values the flexibility it offers regarding profit distribution among partners.

Final Thoughts

Understanding the world of LLC taxation can seem like walking through a maze, but it doesn't have to be overly complicated. This chapter explains the options available for those of you thinking about sole proprietorship taxes. If you're running an LLC solo, choosing to be taxed as a sole proprietor might make your life easier when tax season rolls around—fewer forms mean less hassle. But it's not just about simplifying; remember the flip side, like self-employment taxes and the potential for personal liability. Balancing the ease of reporting with possible financial risks is relevant. So, as you weigh your options, think about what's best for your financial situation and your business's needs.

In the next chapter, we will show the different forms and how you can address filing requirements and meet the deadlines.

Chapter 3: Filing Requirements and Deadlines

Filing taxes for an LLC isn't just about crunching numbers—it's fundamental to keeping your business healthy and thriving. Whether you're new to running an LLC or have been operating for a while, you have to know how your filing requirements and deadlines can mean the difference between smooth sailing and getting caught in a storm of penalties. It's all about knowing what needs to be filed and when so that your business stays on the right side of tax regulations and retains its good standing. This chapter focuses on these essentials, helping you steer clear of costly mistakes to keep your financial plans on track.

You will also find insights into the tax obligations specific to LLCs and the various forms that LLC owners need to be familiar with.

Annual Filing Requirements

When starting or managing an LLC, you need to understand what must be filed annually so you can avoid penalties and maintain good standing with the state. Let's get into the essential annual filings for LLCs so you won't be caught off guard by unexpected fines or compliance issues.

Understanding Required Forms

Firstly, you have to grasp which forms are necessary so you can protect your business. Each state has its specific requirements, so it's important to know exactly which forms apply to your LLC. Missing even a single required filing can result in fines and, in severe cases, personal liability for members if the LLC's protections are compromised. While a state income tax return might come to mind, don't forget that state annual reports are usually separate requirements. This distinction means you have to file each one individually, even if they seem similar at first glance (Fernando, 2024).

Importance of Annual Reports

Annual reports are fundamental for your LLC's compliance strategy. They're much more than paperwork since they maintain your business licenses and credibility. Most states need these reports because they include critical information about your business, such as the names or addresses of your registered agent and management team. This process keeps the public informed about your company's status and operations and helps keep transparency. Plus, for LLCs operating in multiple states, failing to submit an annual report could risk losing the ability to do business outside your home state, complicating matters and possibly leading to the loss of lucrative contracts (Enright, 2021).

Consequences of Missing Deadlines

Now, let's focus on the consequences of missing deadlines. Simply put, late or missed filings don't just come with financial penalties, even if they are a common repercussion. If your business is no longer considered in good standing due to missed reports, you may face risks like being unable to secure loans or expand operations. Even more severely, your LLC could face dissolution by the home state, which means removing your right to do business there and leaving you without limited liability protection should legal issues arise. For example, if you're trying to sue someone or enter contracts when your business credibility is already jeopardized, this would be tough, to say the least.

Strategies for Staying Organized

So, how do you avoid these costly mistakes? For one, understanding the forms needed and their deadlines is a great start, but keeping organized allows you to meet all obligations on time. Use tracking tools or set reminders well before deadlines so you know you're covered. Some businesses use services that handle compliance filings to focus more on growth rather than paperwork. An organized strategy can save you the headache and expense of filing late or correcting mistakes.

Let's just do a quick summary of why you should stay on top of your annual filings. First, knowing which forms need filing prevents unnecessary penalties and keeps you aligned with state-specific demands. Secondly, knowing the value of yearly reports beyond mere formality preserves your LLC's legitimacy and operational capability. Lastly, diligent organization and timely submissions shield your business from the significant downfalls that come with missed deadlines.

Understanding Form 8832

For many small business owners and aspiring entrepreneurs, figuring out the intricacies of tax obligations can significantly impact the financial health of an LLC.

Purpose of Form 8832

One critical form often associated with LLC taxation is Form 8832. With this, you can use an eligible entity to choose how it will be classified for federal tax purposes: as a corporation, partnership, or an entity disregarded as separate from its owner (*LLC Filing as a Corporation or Partnership*, 2024). Understanding this form's importance is necessary to efficiently manage your LLC's tax obligations.

However, it's just as important to know the tax classification of the form. Without filing this form, an LLC defaults to specific classifications based on its structure. This means that a single-member LLC becomes a "disregarded entity," taxed as if it were a sole proprietorship, and multiple-member LLCs default to partnerships unless otherwise elected. These default settings can have a negative impact. For example, being classified as a disregarded entity means that business income and expenses are reported directly on the owner's personal tax return, so you no longer have personal protection (*What Is a Disregarded Entity?*, 2024).

Picking the right classification with Form 8832 can also help streamline IRS submissions. This can be done by providing clarity on which tax forms and schedules you need to prepare. If an LLC chooses to be treated as a corporation, it must file a corporate tax return using forms like 1120 or 1120S, depending on whether it's an S-corp or C-corp election. This decision affects what paperwork is required and also your overall tax strategy.

Filing Process

Following proper filing steps for Form 8832 will prevent costly mistakes. Any errors or mistakes can cause delays and lead to IRS penalties. So, before filing, make sure you collect your documents. This is the information you will need:

- your LLC structure

- who owns the business

- which tax classification you want

Errors or omissions might lead to processing delays or penalties, so it's thoughtful to gather all necessary information beforehand. Double-checking entries against these requirements before submission reduces the chance of mistakes and ensures that your choice of classification goes into effect without a hitch.

Document Preparation

Start by filling out Form 8832 with the required documents. Understand your LLC structure—how your limited liability company is organized. Check if your LLC is single-member, multi-member, or has elected corporate treatment. Single-member LLCs are typically treated as disregarded entities, while multi-member LLCs are partnerships unless they elect otherwise. Then identify the owners of the business. This information establishes control for tax purposes. With multiple owners, document ownership percentages and roles. This affects how the LLC is taxed. Owners with larger shares may have different tax obligations than other members.

Next, determine your preferred tax classification. Form 8832 lets you choose your business's federal tax treatment. You can select taxation as a sole proprietorship, partnership, or corporation; each option has distinct advantages. An LLC taxed as an S corporation may reduce self-employment taxes, while partnerships offer more flexibility in profit-sharing.

Accuracy Matters

After gathering documents and information, focus on accurate entries. Mistakes can cause processing delays or IRS penalties. Check your entries against requirements. Verify names, addresses, and identification numbers. Small errors can create significant problems. Review your tax classification choice. Make sure it supports your business goals. S corporation status might work well if you want liability protection without double taxation. If you prefer simplicity with less paperwork, staying a disregarded entity could be better.

Filing Process

Fill out Form 8832 and include your LLC's name, address, and Employer Identification Number (EIN). If you lack an EIN, apply through the IRS website or Form SS-4.

Mark your chosen tax classification clearly and inform all members about this choice since it affects future tax obligations. Multi-member LLCs may need all members' signatures. Check the completed form for accuracy, as missing information delays processing. Have someone else review your form to catch oversights. Submit Form 8832 to the IRS electronically or by mail. If mailing, keep copies and use certified mail for tracking. This record will help protect you during submission disputes.

Organization and attention to detail help process your filing efficiently, and these steps help avoid common business owner mistakes.

Remember, proper preparation creates a strong foundation for your business.

When to Elect Tax Status

The timing of your election can align your LLC's tax status with its business plan, and this can optimize deductions and compliance with upcoming fiscal strategies. Suppose you're aware that your LLC will incur substantial start-up losses in its initial phases. Electing a tax status that allows these losses to flow through to the owners' personal returns can lead to valuable tax savings.

You also have to be proactive about when to file, as this can help avoid any nasty surprises come tax season. An election made on Form 8832 applies retroactively to two months and 15 days prior to filing, allowing some flexibility in timing. However, once you've filed your election, there's typically a 60-month "cool down" period before you can change your election again unless the election accompanies a new entity formation.

A Real-World Example

Here's a practical example: a tech startup with an LLC structure. If you expect first-year expenses to exceed income, S Corporation tax status could help. This status passes losses directly to personal tax returns. Form 8832 makes this election, letting losses reduce your tax liability.

Professional Guidance

Talk to a tax professional first. They'll review your situation and recommend the best tax status based on projected revenue and expenses. Then complete Form 8832 with your LLC details and tax status choice. Submit it on time to get retroactive benefits.

Strategic Planning

Good planning affects your tax burden. Project your business performance and research available deductions before selecting a tax status. If you plan major investments or expenses that will cause early-year losses, pick a status that allows those losses to offset other income.

Think about large expenses like office rent or software investments. These startup costs add up fast. The correct tax status turns these early losses into tax savings, supporting your business finances.

Filing Steps

Gather your LLC documents, including operating agreements and financial forecasts. Fill out Form 8832 with your LLC name, address, and tax status choice. Review everything for accuracy to prevent processing delays. Submit your form to the IRS and save a copy. Record the submission date—it determines your retroactive period. Track your election's progress through the IRS or your tax advisor.

Long-Term Effects

Know how your tax choice affects future planning. Each status has specific rules and benefits. S Corporation status offers loss deduction flexibility but needs detailed record-keeping. Track all income, expenses, and distributions carefully.

Watch for tax law changes that might affect your status. Business conditions change, influencing how tax statuses work. Stay informed and work with your advisor to keep your tax strategy aligned with business goals. Timing your LLC's tax status election shapes your financial future. Success comes from understanding your needs and options. Professional advice and careful planning help you make smart tax decisions as your business grows.

Impact on Tax Liabilities

The right tax classification for your LLC leads to substantial tax savings and prevents potential penalties for misclassification. When an LLC inadvertently misses making an election and defaults to a certain classification, it might find itself subject to higher taxes than necessary or face complications when claiming deductions. Taking control over classification decisions via Form 8832 helps your business match tax obligations to your company's needs and plans.

Suppose your LLC anticipates significant growth and plans to reinvest profits. In that case, choosing corporate status might allow funds to be retained within the business at a potentially lower corporate tax rate, rather than facing immediate distribution taxation at the individual level. Filing Form 8832 shapes your tax foundation. It's not just paperwork; it's a tool to tailor your LLC's tax infrastructure, aligning it with both present needs and future aspirations.

Consider this situation: your LLC expects major growth soon. Corporate status might help here. As a corporation, your LLC can keep earnings inside the company. You can reinvest these funds for growth while paying lower corporate tax rates. This strategy beats distributing profits to owners who pay higher individual tax rates. Also, keeping profits in the business offers practical advantages. You can use the money for development, research, or expansion without the immediate tax cost of owner distributions. Smart tax classification choices help your business grow without unnecessary costs.

Form 8832 lets you control your business's financial structure. Your tax choice affects tax payments, distributions, liabilities, and deductions. Know what each classification means and how it supports your strategy.

When completing Form 8832, think about your current business state and future plans. The form needs specific information: entity name, desired classification, and classification start date. These details set your LLC's tax duties and benefits. Accurate information prevents future problems.

Your LLC's tax classification has lasting effects. Form 8832 helps match your tax obligations to your needs. This planning can cut tax costs and improve reinvestment options. A solid tax foundation helps your business handle financial changes better.

Multi-Member LLC Filing

Let's start by looking at an important choice: whether your LLC should be classified as a partnership or corporation for tax purposes. This will have an impact on how your business income gets treated by the IRS.

Tax Classification Options

You already know that depending on what structure you choose, there are different advantages and disadvantages. However, it's worth spending some time weighing the pros and cons of each classification option to see which aligns best with your business strategy and financial goals.

Form 1065 Requirements

Once you've settled on the classification, you must turn your attention to Form 1065, which is important to fulfill your tax obligations. The IRS requires multi-member LLCs categorized as partnerships to file Form 1065 annually. This form reports all financial activities and operations of the partnership throughout the year. Each member receives a Schedule K-1 from the LLC. This form details their share of the company's income, deductions, and credits. The information on Schedule K-1 directly affects each member's personal tax returns, so having it accurate is indispensable (The Investopedia Team, 2024).

Given the importance of Form 1065 and Schedule K-1, you must prepare for them. Begin early, compile the necessary financial records, and consider consulting a tax advisor if you have any doubts. Paying close attention to deadlines can prevent penalties and keep your business in good standing with the IRS.

Meeting the deadlines for Form 1065 and Schedule K-1 is important. The deadline for filing Form 1065 is usually March 15th, unless this date falls on a weekend or holiday, when the deadline moves to the next business day. Following these dates helps avoid late filing penalties and maintains your business in good standing with the IRS. Using a calendar with reminders helps you avoid missing important deadlines. When filling out Form 1065, ensure it accurately reflects all financial activities. You must report all income received by the partnership, including money from sales, service fees, interest earned, or any other forms of income generated during the year. Besides income, you should also account for various expenses that the partnership has incurred, like operational costs such as rent, utilities, and salaries. Documenting these details helps show an accurate picture of your partnership's financial situation to the IRS.

To complete Form 1065 correctly, you must include information about each partner, including their share of profits and losses. It's necessary to determine each member's ownership percentage honestly. This percentage determines how profits and losses are distributed among the partners. You can establish special allocations if applicable. These special allocations must follow the IRS rules to be valid. After you fill out Form 1065, you must distribute Schedule K-1s to each member of the LLC. It's important that these forms are filled out accurately and promptly. Each member should then use their Schedule K-1 to report their income, deductions, and credits on their personal tax returns. The timing of sending out these forms should align with your overall filing strategy. Schedule K-1s must be distributed to members by the due date of Form 1065.

Take these steps seriously to keep your partnership compliant with IRS requirements. Each phase of preparing and filing Form 1065 and distributing Schedule K-1s works together. When you manage these parts well, you reduce stress and potential issues with the IRS. Planning ahead saves you time and effort, allowing you to focus on growing your business rather than worrying about tax penalties.

Distributing Income and Loss

Now, let's move on to distributing income and losses among LLC members. You must have transparent allocation strategies to ensure satisfaction and fairness and avoid potential disputes among members. Income and losses in an LLC often follow the ownership percentages outlined in the operating agreement. However, specific arrangements might allow for specialized allocations tailored to particular circumstances or member roles (*Beneficial Ownership Information*, n.d.).

Have open discussions about these distributions, as these can improve transparency and promote trust among members. For example, a member who dedicates more time and effort to the business may justifiably receive a larger share. Any arrangements of this nature should be documented clearly within the operating agreement to avoid confusion and conflict down the line.

Record-Keeping Best Practices

Record-keeping is just as important because effective record-keeping practices make financial tracking easier and allow for the accurate filing of tax documents. It helps you keep up with paperwork and helps your business run smoothly while remaining compliant with IRS requirements.

You can start by establishing a system that includes all pertinent financial records, such as receipts, invoices, bank statements, and payroll documents. Digital tools and accounting software can vastly improve organization and accessibility, reducing errors and delays during tax season. Remember to also reconcile accounts regularly to catch discrepancies early on and maintain a clear financial picture of your operations.

Staying organized simplifies tax filing and creates a reliable resource for verifying records and figures on filed forms. Organized documentation can help you in the event of an audit, where transparency and quick access to records can expedite the process and mitigate potential issues.

Federal vs. State Deadlines

Filing taxes as an LLC needs careful attention to deadlines. Missing these often leads to penalties, increased audit risk, or lost benefits, but let's dig into the main differences in filing deadlines.

Understanding Federal Deadlines

To begin with, complying with federal deadlines helps you avoid penalties. The United States has specific tax timelines set by the IRS, which, if not adhered to, can lead to significant financial consequences. For LLCs taxed as partnerships, Form 1065 is due on March 15th (Tuytel, 2024). However, if extra time is needed, you can apply for an extension using Form 7004, pushing the deadline to September 15th. On the other hand, single-member LLCs taxed as sole proprietorships use Schedule C, attached to their personal tax returns, usually due on April 15th. Following these timelines creates clear financial records and helps you plan better for the rest of the fiscal year.

State-Specific Deadlines

State-specific requirements can complicate the situation a little more. This difficulty is because each state has its own rules. For example, California requires LLCs to pay an annual minimum franchise tax by April 15th, while New York mandates biennial statements every two years. If you fail to meet these state deadlines, you can jeopardize the company's good standing, and it might result in administrative dissolution or revocation.

Consequences of Missed Deadlines

Financial penalties often accrue daily until the overdue tax return is filed or the tax owed is paid. Businesses might also lose benefits such as exemptions or credits they would otherwise qualify for. More concerning is the potential increase in audit risk. The IRS and state tax authorities may view late filings as red flags, prompting more frequent and thorough reviews of financial records, which can be both time-consuming and stressful for business owners.

Strategies for Managing Deadlines

Since tracking various deadlines is complex, you need a plan to handle these tasks. Using tax software made for small businesses sends automated reminders, accurate calculations, and even integration with accounting systems to help with the filing process. If you need it, remember to get help from accountants or tax consultants, especially if you are unfamiliar with tax regulations.

Organized planning remains an underrated yet powerful tool. Developing a tax calendar at the beginning of the fiscal year, listing all relevant federal, state, and local filing deadlines, helps keep everything on track. If you set regular internal reviews of financial statements, you will be able to spot discrepancies early and make necessary adjustments before submission.

Final Thoughts

In this chapter, we looked at how you can handle LLC tax filings. You now understand the annual filing requirements that keep your business safe from penalties and in good standing with the state. While paperwork is important, this is more about protecting your business's credibility and making sure that you can continue operating seamlessly, especially if you're expanding across multiple states. We also discussed Form 8832, which is about choosing the right tax classification for your LLC. This decision isn't a small one, as it impacts how your income is treated and aligns with your business strategy.

Let's not forget the differences between federal and state deadlines. Missing these could result in some bad surprises like penalties or even increased audit risk. With all of this said and done, in the next chapter, we will look at another very important part of LLC taxes that can give you the upper hand with your business: maximizing deductions and credits so you can keep more of the money you make.

Chapter 4: Maximizing Deductions and Credits

You can find opportunities within the tax code that can help reduce what you owe. These legal strategies help you manage your business's financial health. In turn, this allows more of your hard-earned money to stay where it belongs—in your pocket or reinvested into your business growth. What's important here is to seek out every viable deduction and credit. When you do this, you're setting your business up for greater success and sustainability. It's like a treasure hunt for your finances, where each deduction or credit found brings you closer to a more favorable fiscal year.

This chapter will explore key tax strategies for small business owners and entrepreneurs. We will also cover essential deductions, such as home office or vehicle expenses, equipment purchases under Section 179, and daily business expenses.

Common Business Deductions for LLCs

Understanding deductible expenses makes a major difference in reducing the financial burdens on LLCs. Some of these deductions can significantly reduce tax liabilities and give you much-needed relief for your business. To begin with, let's look at start-up expenses. When getting your LLC off the ground, costs can quickly pile up. From legal fees to marketing expenses, these initial costs are considered capital investments in your business. The IRS allows you to deduct up to $5,000 of start-up costs in the first year, provided your total start-up costs don't exceed $50,000. If they do, this deduction begins to phase out on a dollar-for-dollar basis. Any remaining costs can be amortized over 15 years (*Deducting Startup and Expansion Costs*, 2017). This strategy improves cash flow management because you can reclaim part of your initial investment sooner rather than later.

Start-Up Expenses

When considering start-up expenses, think about everything that went into launching your LLC. Common expenses include registering your business, hiring staff, leasing office space, and purchasing initial inventory. If you are diligent in tracking these expenses, you can maximize your deductions and improve your early financial standing. Just remember that detailed record-keeping is absolutely essential to substantiate these deductions in case of an audit.

Home Office Deduction

The home office deduction is a valuable tool for LLC owners, and it works by using a portion of their home exclusively for business purposes. This deduction lets you claim a percentage of household expenses proportional to the size of your home office relative to your entire house. These can include utilities, rent or mortgage interest, property taxes, and even home repairs. To qualify, the workspace must be used regularly and exclusively for running your business (Fontinelle, 2024). For example, if your home office takes up 10% of your house's square footage, you might deduct 10% of your home-related expenses.

Vehicle Expenses

The vehicle expenses deduction can also impact your tax savings if you use a car for business purposes. The IRS offers two methods for calculating this deduction: the standard mileage rate and the actual expense method. The standard mileage rate is straightforward; you multiply the business miles driven by a set rate per mile determined annually by the IRS. Meanwhile, the actual expense method requires tallying all vehicle-related expenses, such as gas, insurance, maintenance, and depreciation, and then multiplying the total by the percentage of business use (Hyseni, 2023). You have to consider which of these two methods yields greater tax savings given your specific circumstances.

You can optimize these deductions by keeping thorough records of your vehicle's business use, such as odometer readings, travel dates, and the purpose of each trip. If your car is used for business 80% of the time, you can deduct 80% of the allowable expenses.

Business Equipment and Supplies

Also, consider the deduction opportunities available through business equipment and supplies. For LLCs, purchasing equipment and necessary supplies is an ongoing need. This could be computers, desks, software subscriptions, or industrial machinery. All of these purchases can lower your taxable income. Many of these assets are deductible under Section 179, which allows businesses to deduct the full purchase price of qualifying equipment in the year it is put into service. However, these assets should be used primarily for business purposes, and there are limits on the total amount deducted annually (Hyseni, 2023).

You can also claim everyday operational supplies, known as consumables, such as printer paper, ink, and cleaning supplies. These are entirely deductible as they are used within the year purchased.

Using Tax Credits Effectively

Let's look at some essential tax credits designed to alleviate financial burdens and boost innovation in businesses like yours.

Research and Development Credits

The Research and Development (R&D) Tax Credit is important in promoting innovation. This credit encourages companies to invest in research and development activities within the U.S., ultimately improving competitiveness and economic growth. If a tech startup spends funds on developing new software or conducting groundbreaking research that propels its industry forward, these expenses qualify for substantial tax savings. When partnering with institutions like universities for R&D projects, businesses can claim a portion of these expenditures towards their taxes and promote collaboration that fuels job creation and technological advancements. However, this credit is a bit complex, so businesses should talk with tax professionals to make sure all eligible expenses are accurately reported and claimed (*R&D Tax Credits and Deductions*, 2024).

Work Opportunity Tax Credit

Now, let's move on to the Work Opportunity Tax Credit (WOTC). This credit is another practical tool for businesses that want to reduce their tax liabilities while making impactful hiring decisions. The WOTC incentivizes employers to hire individuals from certain target groups who consistently face significant barriers to employment, such as veterans, ex-felons, or individuals receiving government assistance. For each eligible employee hired, businesses can receive a tax credit, which varies depending on the employee's target group and hours worked—up to $9,600 per qualified hire in some cases. Because of this, WOTC helps reduce tax liability and positively impacts communities by offering opportunities to those who need them most. Businesses can plan strategic recruitment efforts around these criteria to maximize savings while building a diverse and productive workforce.

Energy Efficiency Tax Credits

The Energy Efficiency Tax Credits represent a great way to align financial savings with sustainability goals. With climate change becoming an increasingly pressing issue, many governments offer tax credits to businesses investing in energy-efficient technologies and renewable energy projects. These can include installing solar panels, upgrading to energy-efficient heating and cooling systems, or implementing other eco-friendly technologies that reduce carbon footprints. These investments reduce utility bills and drive down tax obligations while simultaneously improving a company's reputation as an environmentally conscious entity. If you use these energy efficiency upgrades, you can position your company at the forefront of the green movement, potentially drawing eco-conscious customers and investors interested in sustainable practices.

Small Business Health Care Tax Credit

Last, but definitely not least, the Small Business Health Care Tax Credit makes providing health benefits more financially feasible for small employers. For small businesses offering health insurance to employees, this credit reimburses up to 50% of premium costs. To qualify, the business must have fewer than 25 full-time equivalent employees, pay average wages below a specified amount, and cover at least half of the insurance premiums for employees. Offering competitive health benefits attracts talented workers, boosting morale and reducing turnover. Together, these factors contribute to a more stable and loyal workforce.

Small businesses must pay average wages below a certain specified amount. This wage limit depends on the number of employees and changes by the year. Businesses should check available resources about these wage standards to check if they qualify. This requirement directs the benefits to small businesses that need it most. To get the Small Business Health Care Tax Credit, employers must cover at least half of the insurance premiums for their employees. Business owners should share the costs of premiums with their employees. Paying these expenses fulfills the eligibility criteria but also creates a sense of shared responsibility with their employees.

Providing health benefits helps attract talented workers. In a competitive job market, potential employees look for organizations focused on their well-being. Offering health insurance sets you apart from competitors. It shows you value your workforce, which improves recruiting efforts. Besides attracting talent, offering competitive health benefits improves employee morale. When employees know their health needs are taken care of, they feel more satisfied with their jobs. This satisfaction creates higher productivity levels and better overall performance. A happy employee becomes a motivated employee, helping the company's success.

Health benefits reduce employee turnover. When a business invests in its employees, employees often remain loyal to the company. High turnover rates are costly due to recruiting and training new staff. With health benefits, small businesses build an environment that supports retention and long-term employee relationships.

A stable workforce drives the growth of a small business. When employees stay longer, they gain experience and deep knowledge of the company's operations, which increases efficiency. Employers also benefit from continuity in their workforce, which improves teamwork and collaboration.

Small businesses can start by reviewing their current health insurance options and finding affordable plans for employees. Working with health insurance brokers who know small business needs shows available options. These professionals guide small business owners through the market, find suitable plans, and calculate costs. Once you choose a plan, business owners can tell their employees about the insurance. Clear communication about the plan benefits, how claims work, and what employees need to do to enroll increases participation. It's important to explain the plan, so employees understand the value of the benefits.

Small businesses should stay current with changes in tax law or healthcare regulations. Knowing how these changes impact the business and its employees. Learning how to adjust policies or benefits based on specific needs or regulations helps maintain compliance and continue providing valuable benefits to staff.

Using the Small Business Health Care Tax Credit, small business owners can better offer health benefits and build an environment that supports loyalty and stability. This shows the importance that health care plays in employees' lives and promotes overall well-being within the workplace. Investing in health insurance becomes an investment in the future of the business. Supporting employee health creates a strong foundation that promotes growth, engagement, and long-term success. As small business owners handle the complexities of providing benefits, the tax credit becomes a helpful tool to make this important offering more attainable and manageable.

Record-Keeping for Deductions

Thorough documentation is one of the most important aspects of reducing tax liabilities and safeguarding against potential audits. Accurate record-keeping is an important component of this strategy, which is both a shield and a strategy for small business owners, entrepreneurs, and self-employed individuals.

Importance of Accurate Record-Keeping

Accurate record-keeping helps prevent missed deductions and mitigates audit risks. When records are meticulously maintained, they show an authoritative account of all business transactions. This attention to detail means that no deduction goes unnoticed or unclaimed, potentially saving you thousands of dollars annually. Well-organized records reduce the stress and complexities associated with audits. If the IRS decides to examine your returns, having complete and accurate documents at hand will make the process much less scary.

Methods for Organizing Receipts

A great way to manage your records, especially when dealing with numerous receipts, is through organized digital systems. Keeping paper receipts in shoeboxes makes tax preparation harder than necessary. Instead, you can use digital tools to organize your receipts to simplify the tax preparation process. There are various software solutions that allow you to scan and categorize receipts digitally. These tools often come with features that let you tag transactions, making it easier to retrieve necessary documents during tax season. Keep your receipts sorted by category or date, so you will spot every deductible expense quickly.

Maintaining Financial Records

Keeping detailed financial records helps you follow tax and grow your business. Doing this can be a great help when it comes to accurate financial reports such as balance sheets and income statements. These documents are invaluable for compliance purposes and if you're looking to seek funding or investment. Well-organized records show that you are reliable and have a transparent business, which instills confidence in lenders or investors. Also, these records offer insights into your business's financial health, which, in turn, allows informed decision-making that can spur growth and expansion.

Using Software for Tracking

Using software to track expenses improves both accuracy and efficiency. Software tools give you easy-to-use interfaces and functionalities that meet modern business needs. They automatically sync with bank accounts and categorize transactions, giving you a comprehensive view of your financial activity. When it comes to automating mundane tasks, these tools allow you to focus more on strategic planning instead of manual data entry. Most of these tools also back up essential data, which provides security against potential data loss. The integration of technology alleviates administrative burdens and can assist you in maintaining compliance standards.

All of this helps you establish a solid system for documentation, which helps maximize tax benefits. This could be done by keeping meticulous records, organizing receipts via digital means, or using dedicated software for tracking. Each one of these methods contributes to a solid documentation framework. For small business owners and entrepreneurs, this translates into fewer headaches during tax season and more opportunities for financial optimization throughout the year. When you prioritize thorough documentation, you know that you're capturing every possible deduction, staying compliant, and setting the foundation for ongoing business success.

Creating a solid documentation system helps increase tax benefits. This means keeping thorough records and managing receipts well through digital means or tracking software. When you digitize your receipts, you clear physical space and keep multiple backups of your important documents. You can take photos of paper receipts and upload them to your software, which removes the risk of losing them as paper fades or tears. Some software solutions allow you to scan receipts directly into their system, which speeds up the entire process.

For small business owners and entrepreneurs, detailed documentation means fewer headaches during tax season. When tax time arrives, you want to feel prepared, not panicked. Instead of scrambling to piece together your financial records at the last minute, having everything in one software tool creates a smoother, less stressful process. This preparedness opens up more opportunities for financial optimization throughout the year. Knowing your spending habits and financial patterns helps you make informed decisions about where to cut costs or where to invest more resources. When you focus on thorough documentation and use effective tracking software, you catch every possible deduction. This means you don't miss any tax benefits that could save you money. Staying compliant with tax regulations prevents issues with tax authorities and helps you build a stronger financial foundation. It builds transparency in your business dealings and improves your credibility with investors or financial institutions.

Expense-tracking software has become a modern necessity. Its accuracy, efficiency, and security significantly improve financial management. To achieve smoother financial management, spend time finding the right tool for your business and making it part of your daily operations. This approach improves your business's financial health and helps you achieve long-term goals with less stress.

Avoiding Missed Tax Opportunities

Tax deductions require more than knowing the right forms to fill out. They also require strategic planning and awareness of what can cause mistakes.

Understanding Tax Deadlines

Understanding tax deadlines helps businesses optimize their deductions and credits. Missing these crucial deadlines can jeopardize potential savings. Late filings often result in penalties, interest charges, and missed deductions that could have reduced your tax liability. To stay ahead, mark due dates on calendars and set reminders. A practical approach could be to complete your filings well before the deadline, giving ample time for unexpected issues or needed clarifications.

Common Oversights by Small Businesses

Small businesses often experience common oversights during tax filing, which can halt optimal tax preparation. One major issue lies in inaccurate record-keeping. Inadequate records often lead to valuable deductions slipping through the cracks or being altogether missed. That's why setting up a reliable tracking system is so important. Using accounting software or hiring a professional bookkeeper adds a layer of accuracy that minimizes risks, but when you maintain meticulous records of income, expenses, and receipts, you can streamline the entire tax filing process.

Misclassification of workers is another frequent misstep that can carry hefty penalties. Many small business owners struggle with distinguishing between employees and independent contractors, yet proper classification is needed to comply with IRS regulations. Confusion here can lead to unexpected back taxes and legal issues. Hence, understanding IRS criteria for worker classification. If you're unsure, consulting with a professional can save future headaches and potential financial setbacks.

Consulting Tax Professionals

Businesses shouldn't overlook the value of consulting tax professionals. While it might seem like just another expense, professional guidance often uncovers overlooked deductions and credits that can minimize tax liabilities. Tax consultants are updated with current laws and understand how to navigate the complexities of tax codes efficiently. They provide insights into industry-specific deductions that may not be widely known.

Investing in expert advice can pay dividends by preventing errors that could lead to penalties.

Regular Tax Strategy Reviews

Regular tax strategy reviews should become a cornerstone of business operations. The tax landscape is always changing, with new laws and amendments cropping up regularly. What was deductible last year might not be applicable today—or vice versa—and because of that, you should periodically review this so you can adapt your strategies effectively, make room to add new deductions as they emerge, and drop outdated practices.

Tax strategy reviews do more than keep up with changes; they reflect business growth or operational changes. For instance, hiring additional staff, expanding operations, or launching new product lines can impact your tax situation. Updating tax plans to accommodate these changes means obligations are met and opportunities for deductions or credits are successfully applied.

Understanding tax deadlines and doing regular assessments builds a strong foundation for effective tax management. This matters most to self-employed individuals whose unique circumstances demand customized strategies. Entrepreneurs and startups also benefit immensely from this practice, as it allows them to pivot and adjust quickly without being bogged down by avoidable errors.

Bringing It All Together

We've covered many different strategies that can reduce the tax burden for LLCs, from start-up costs to home office deductions. This ensures you don't leave money on the table when it comes to your taxes, and for those of you who have been setting up your operations or are in the thick of the business hustle, these tips can seriously beef up your savings. Keeping an eye on your expenses and knowing what can be deducted can make a difference in your financial health as you set up shop or continue to grow.

Tax credits improve your bottom line in addition to deductions. We've shown how incentives like R&D credits or energy efficiency programs can serve double duty by saving taxes and promoting broader goals like innovation and sustainability. Next, we will discuss tracking and organizing your business's expenses, which we've mentioned. Because of its importance, we really need to go into detail about it.

Chapter 5: Tracking and Organizing Business Expenses

Tracking and organizing business expenses is one of the most important aspects of running a successful business. It's about keeping tabs on your spending as well as having a system that supports growth and facilitates smart financial choices. For many small business owners, managing expenses is like juggling a complex puzzle. Yet, mastering this skill paves the way to better financial stability and compliance with tax regulations. Whether you're just starting out or looking to refine your approach, understanding how to efficiently track and organize expenses can drastically affect your bottom line and open up new opportunities for savings and investment.

Here, we will go through various methods that help you keep your financial records in top shape. You'll explore how you can implement expense tracking software, which can transform how you manage finances by automating processes and reducing errors. This chapter also uncovers ways to customize these tools to fit your unique business needs better.

Implementing Expense Tracking Software

Choosing the right software can really change the way you manage your expenses efficiently. Many options exist, but not all software is created equal. One of the main aspects to consider is integration capabilities. Choosing expense-tracking software that works seamlessly with your existing accounting systems reduces redundant data entry. This means you spend less time manually transferring data between platforms and more time focusing on what matters—growing your business. Integrated systems often lead to fewer errors since they automate the data flow between tools, improving accuracy and streamlining operations—an important factor for maintaining up-to-date financial records.

Setting up the System

Another feature to look out for in expense tracking software is customization. Generic solutions might not address the needs of your business, but software that offers customization options allows you to get the features that fit your specific requirements. For example, being able to categorize expenses according to your business's structure or industry-specific needs can give you better insights when reviewing your spending. Custom categories can simplify the process of tracking different types of expenses, such as travel, office supplies, or client meals, which ultimately leads to better management and control over your financial resources.

Utilizing Reporting Features

Another aspect to consider is using reporting tools embedded within the software. Advanced reporting features allow you to unlock valuable information about your spending patterns, helping you manage your budget more effectively. When you analyze these detailed reports, you can identify areas where you're overspending and adjust accordingly. These reports can also help pinpoint seasonal trends in your expenses, facilitating more accurate budget forecasts and financial planning. Also, having access to real-time data via these reports allows you to make informed decisions quickly.

Regular Software Review

Check your software regularly to track its cost-effectiveness. As your business grows and changes, your software needs will too. Review if the software meets your business demands. If your company is growing, you may need to upgrade to a more comprehensive tool that can handle increased transaction volumes or offer more sophisticated analytics. Keeping an eye on updates or new features released by the software provider can also improve functionality and user experience. You can also stay informed about software pricing or licensing changes to manage costs effectively and know that you're getting the best value for your investment.

While exploring these options, remember that integrating new software into your business processes should be as non-disruptive as possible. Businesses often face initial resistance when adopting new technology, primarily due to the learning curve involved. Therefore, opting for software with a user-friendly interface can reduce training time and facilitate smoother adoption among team members. Simplified navigation and clear instructions can increase overall productivity, allowing your staff to adapt quickly without extensive downtime.

Selecting platforms with mobile apps can give you the added benefit of on-the-go expense tracking. Recording expenses immediately as they occur—even from a mobile device—can prevent discrepancies and help with accurate record-keeping. Mobile apps typically include intuitive interfaces designed for quick information entry and retrieval, which can be particularly useful for employees who travel frequently.

It's also important to mention the role of scalability and automation in choosing the right expense-tracking software. As your business grows, the software should grow with you, accommodating more users, transactions, and enhanced functionalities without compromising performance. Automation features such as approval workflows or automated notifications can save valuable time by reducing manual interventions, thereby improving workflow efficiency.

Categorizing Business Expenses

When you organize business expenses well, you facilitate financial management and improve insight into spending patterns. Setting up common categories gives you a structured framework that simplifies financial reporting and maintains compliance with regulatory standards. You'll see which areas consume the most resources and where savings can be achieved.

Using Tags and Labels

A great starting point is setting up an effective categorization system. This involves creating broad categories that cover different types of expenses, such as rent, utilities, travel, and office supplies. Within these broad categories, subcategories can be defined to capture more specific details. For example, travel expenses might be further divided into airfare, lodging, meals, and transportation. This granularity allows for better tracking of individual spending elements and helps in understanding where adjustments can be made.

Using tagging or labeling systems improves how you analyze expense reports. Tags can be used to highlight important aspects like the purpose of an expense, the department responsible, or even the project linked to it. They also help filter through large amounts of data, making it easier to highlight significant trends or outliers. This system works particularly well for startups and growing businesses tracking their financial health, especially since minute details can often reveal larger opportunities for cost optimization.

Establishing Accountable Systems

Accountability is another aspect of efficient expense categorization that you should look into. Having a financial manager within your organization keeps categorization techniques in check. This designated person would oversee expense reports, train employees on proper expense categorization, and conduct regular audits to catch any discrepancies. With someone specifically monitoring this process, businesses can maintain accuracy, reduce errors, and uphold compliance with organizational policies and external regulations.

Adapting Categories Seasonally

You shouldn't overlook the importance of adapting categorization methods based on seasonal changes either. Financial strategies need to evolve with time, and being responsive to temporary costs during certain months or seasons can help in planning for budget fluctuations. For example, a retailer might see increased shipping costs during the holiday season, so having a category specifically for December logistics could highlight these spikes and prompt proactive budgeting measures moving forward. Similarly, summer might bring higher air conditioning bills for office spaces, which should be accounted for in expense forecasts.

Real business stories show how good expense tracking makes a difference. Consider a bakery that identified its artisanal ingredient costs through careful categorization. This allows them to adjust pricing strategies to protect profits without sacrificing quality. Likewise, a freelance graphic designer traveling the world noticed through her categorization system that her frequent flights and accommodations were eating into her bottom line. This insight prompted her to adjust her travel strategy and budget accordingly.

AI and automated tools change how businesses handle their finances. These tools can automatically sort expenses into predetermined categories using machine learning algorithms. They analyze vendor details, purchase descriptions, and transaction times, refining their accuracy over time. Automation reduces manual work, maintains consistency, and lowers the risk of human error in financial records. Business owners can use these technologies to improve their categorization processes, creating better alignment between actual expenses and their recorded categories (Behrani, n.d.).

Even with greater technology, keeping a degree of human oversight matters. Check and update your categorization system to keep it relevant to business needs. Categories might change as new expenses arise or old ones become obsolete. You should also run regular audits and cross-checks to make sure that the automatic systems work correctly and fix any anomalies promptly.

Maintaining Audit-Ready Records

Every small business owner, entrepreneur, and budding tax consultant knows that preparing for potential audits is a good practice and absolutely instrumental. When the time comes for audits, having well-prepared records can save you a lot of headaches, time, and even money.

Record Retention Policies

First thing's first: developing clear retention policies. This means understanding how long you need to keep each type of document to comply with legal requirements. Such policies are important because they help avoid unnecessary clutter and make sure that your records are always ready when needed. For instance, financial records often have varying retention periods. Tax documents might need to be kept for seven years, while payroll records could require a different timeline. Knowing these specifics helps streamline your documentation efforts and keeps your business compliant with regulations (Iron Mountain, 2024).

Creating Organized Folders

Organize both digital and physical storage systems. Set up your files like a library where every book has its place and label. With cloud storage or physical filing cabinets, consistent labeling and organization speed up retrieval during an audit. A well-labeled folder system makes it easier for auditors and helps you or your staff quickly find necessary documents without stress. Consider adopting an electronic document management system (EDMS) to automate organization, allowing you to categorize files by type, year, or other customizable tags. This system cuts down on search time and improves efficiency (*NOW CFO Ranks on the 2024 Inc. 5000*, n.d.).

Documenting Expenses

One of the main requirements for preparing for audits is meticulously documenting every expense. You will need to keep more than receipts; you must build a clear trail of evidence for every transaction. Having both physical copies and digital scans creates redundancy that guards against loss and facilitates easy access. Digital copies are particularly useful because they can be indexed and searched through EDMS tools, which lowers paper clutter and prevents critical documents from slipping through the cracks. Recording all expenses proves transactions and leaves little room for discrepancies during audits.

Preparing for Potential Audits

You should implement pre-audit strategies, as running practice audits recreates the experience and reveals weaknesses in your record-keeping processes. Think of them as dress rehearsals, showing you what to expect and where to improve before the real deal comes around. Also, maintaining detailed process records gives auditors a roadmap of your internal workings and demonstrates transparency and readiness. Keeping current with these records shows current practices and adherence to controls set out to maintain compliance. These steps tell auditors of your commitment to accurate and honest reporting, thus making the actual audit smoother and potentially less intrusive (*NOW CFO Ranks on the 2024 Inc. 5000*, n.d.).

You need to be diligent and adapt to new regulations and best practices. Learning of any changes to laws affecting your industry or state keeps your retention policies effective and relevant. Review your policies regularly to accommodate changing needs, technological advancements, and regulatory updates. Consider consulting legal experts who can alert you to new requirements and help safeguard your operations against compliance lapses.

Improve your audit preparation by following a thorough documentation process. Make sure each step in your operational processes has clear records. When you have a financial procedure with multiple steps, document each step clearly and include responsible parties. During an audit, you can find the relevant documentation. This preparedness aids auditors and strengthens your internal accountability. Regular training sessions for your team on compliance and auditing standards improve your organization's readiness. Training employees about best practices and current laws helps them make informed decisions in their daily tasks. It creates a culture of compliance throughout the organization. If everyone understands accurate record-keeping and compliance, the company becomes better equipped for an audit.

You should set specific timelines for regular audits of your own processes. Running internal reviews periodically helps catch discrepancies or issues before they become larger problems. Create a schedule for these internal reviews and stick to it. You might conduct an internal audit every quarter. During these reviews, assess all aspects of your operation, from financial records to operational procedures. This approach prepares you for external audits and improves your overall efficiency.

Start by creating a checklist for the audit process. Before the actual audit starts, use this checklist to confirm all necessary documents and records are ready for review. Create categories for different types of documents and set deadlines for each to be completed. Include sections for financial statements, compliance records, and human resources documents. This organized method makes gathering information simpler. Work with your auditors during the process. Communication matters. When auditors review your records, be open to discussing your processes. This approach helps establish a good relationship with the auditing team. It shows your organization values transparency and welcomes feedback. Good communication clarifies points of confusion and reduces the time spent on the audit.

Preparing for an audit means laying the groundwork, which requires thoughtful planning, documentation, and communication. Running practice audits, keeping detailed records, and staying informed about regulatory changes help position your organization for success. Working with legal experts and conducting regular reviews of your practices enhances your preparedness. Taking these steps helps you create a culture of compliance that strengthens your organization.

Troubleshooting Common Tracking Issues

Tracking and organizing business expenses can be a challenging task for small business owners, entrepreneurs, and self-employed individuals.

Addressing Inaccurate Entries

One of the first hurdles is dealing with inaccurate entries, which can arise from oversight or manual errors during data entry. To address this issue effectively, it's important to verify expense entries against bank statements. This step allows you to check every transaction recorded and if these align with actual financial activity so you can quickly identify and correct discrepancies. Implementing error detection alerts within your accounting software can act as an extra safety net, automatically flagging any anomalies for review before they escalate into bigger issues.

Managing Overlooked Expenses

Another common challenge is capturing those sneaky, overlooked expenses. Oftentimes, these small or nonrecurring expenses are forgotten, leading to incomplete financial records. You should have routine reviews to make sure you're not missing any of these expenses. Setting aside time weekly or monthly to examine all transactions helps spot any missed entries and incorporate them into your financial logs. Building consistent tracking habits matters just as much. Using digital tools or apps that help with on-the-go recording makes tracking expenses easier when they are noted right at the point of expenditure.

Dealing With Software Glitches

For resolving software glitches, regular maintenance should be your priority. Outdated software leads to inefficiencies and even data loss. Keep your software running well by doing regular updates on all financial management software. These updates often come with bug fixes and improvements that improve functionality. In the event software issues persist, you can use customer support resources. Most software providers offer great support options, including tutorials, FAQs, and direct helplines to assist users in troubleshooting their problems swiftly and efficiently. Following these practices resolves current glitches and prepares businesses to handle future issues better.

Navigating Changes in Tax Laws

Learning about tax law changes is vital for maintaining compliance with regulatory standards. Tax laws change frequently, impacting how businesses should manage and report their expenses. Updating your tracking systems to reflect these changes helps avoid penalties and keeps your business in line with the latest regulations. Also, subscribing to newsletters or alerts from trusted tax advisory services can provide timely updates about these legal shifts.

The importance of regular software review becomes apparent when considering the dynamic nature of expense management. As businesses grow, so do their needs for software capabilities. Check whether your current tools meet your company's demands, as it can save time and money in the long run. Review the performance and features of your software to support efficient expense management, creating an environment where financial oversight is both streamlined and effective.

Summary and Reflections

This chapter has looked at some necessary tools and tricks for efficient expense tracking and record management. For example, choosing the right software can save you loads of time by seamlessly integrating with your existing systems, reducing errors, and letting you focus on expanding your business. Customization options allow you to use expense categories that fit your unique needs, providing insights that are important for financial health. And who can forget the power of advanced reporting tools? They give you a clear view of where your money is going, allowing for better budget forecasts and more informed decisions.

Remember, regular checks on your chosen software's effectiveness make a massive difference. Technology changes, and so should your tools to keep fitting your growing business demands. A user-friendly interface and mobile app compatibility allow for a smooth adoption within your team, while scalability and automation keep pace with your expanding operations. Lastly, don't forget the value of ongoing evaluation so your expense tracking methods continue to serve your needs effectively, making those audits far less daunting and your record-keeping rock-solid. In the next chapter, we will be looking at the impact of pass-through taxation and how this can help your business grow.

Chapter 6: Pass-Through Taxation Impact

P ass-through taxation is a fascinating topic for anyone getting into the world of business ownership, especially for those considering setting up an LLC. Initially, it might seem like just another layer of complexity in the already thorny world of taxes, but it's actually a very important concept that can simplify life for small business owners. When you understand this form of taxation, you can find ways to optimize your tax situation and make smarter financial decisions from day one. Pass-through taxation shifts the burden of paying taxes from the company itself to its individual members, which allows income to be taxed at the personal level rather than the corporate level. This seemingly small shift can have significant effects on your tax responsibilities and savings.

This chapter explains pass-through taxation by breaking down how it works for different business structures like sole proprietorships, partnerships, LLCs, and S corporations. We discuss the mechanics of reporting income and expenses on your tax returns as either a single-member or multi-member LLC. You will find details about benefits such as avoiding double taxation and making use of business losses while touching on critical aspects like self-employment taxes and retirement planning. Understanding state variations will give you a complete picture to make sure there is compliance and optimal tax efficiency. All of this is practical knowledge that affects your bottom line.

How Pass-Through Taxation Works

Here's how the mechanics of pass-through taxation work for LLC owners. This form of taxation can simplify tax obligations and lower liabilities for business owners. Essentially, pass-through taxation implies that any profits earned by an LLC aren't taxed at the company level. Instead, these profits are passed through to individual members, who then report the income on their personal tax returns. This shift in liability from the business to individuals effectively reduces overall tax burdens, making it appealing for small businesses and startups.

Let me give you a quick example. Say that you run a successful graphic design LLC that earned $120,000 in 2023. If you use pass-through taxation, your LLC doesn't pay corporate taxes on this income. The entire $120,000 "passes through" to your personal tax return using Schedule C of Form 1040. If you're in the 24% tax bracket, you only pay taxes once at your personal rate, instead of having to face both corporate tax (which would be at 21%) and then personal tax on distributions.

Basic Mechanic

Another advantage of pass-through entities is their ability to avoid double taxation, which we explained above with an example. However, let's have a closer look at how the mechanics really work. In a traditional corporation setup, income is taxed twice: first at the corporate level when the company makes a profit, and then again at the individual level when dividends are distributed to shareholders. Pass-through status circumvents this by taxing income only at the individual owner's level, offering potential savings, and simplifying tax processes (Kagan, 2024).

This strategy is excellent for making informed decisions about your business. Knowing how your income will be taxed allows you to better plan for expenses, investments, and even expansion opportunities. It also allows for a more strategic approach to managing finances, ensures compliance with tax law, and maximizes savings in the long run.

Pass-Through Eligibility

Now, which business structures qualify for pass-through status? Typically, sole proprietorships, partnerships, LLCs, and S corporations stand under this umbrella. Each structure has its differences, but they share the commonality of income being reported directly on personal tax filings rather than at an entity level (Coombes, 2023). This understanding allows business owners to choose the right entity based on their needs and goals, facilitating effective tax planning and decision-making.

To paint a clearer picture, let's consider how pass-through taxation unfolds within LLCs:

For single-member LLCs, the process resembles that of a sole proprietorship. Here, income and expenses are reported using Form 1040 Schedule C. The individual owner carries the burden of reporting all profits and losses on their personal return, bypassing the need for a separate corporate filing.

Impact on Business Operations

On the other hand, multi-member LLCs are treated similarly to partnerships. Members receive a Schedule K-1 outlining their share of the LLC's income, deductions, and credits, which they must then report on their personal tax returns. The LLC also files Form 1065, a partnership information return, detailing how revenue was distributed among members. This lack of entity-level taxation reinforces the benefits of choosing an LLC structure for many entrepreneurs.

Recognizing which business entity aligns with one's operational goals and financial strategy can dramatically impact tax efficiency. For example, some LLCs opt for S corporation status to benefit from possible payroll tax savings without affecting pass-through treatment. Business owners can customize their choices so they can pick the best fit for their circumstances and future plans.

State Variations

That said, while pass-through taxation has numerous advantages, variations based on state regulations exist. Each state might impose different requirements or taxes, such as franchise taxes or fees, which can impact the overall benefit of this tax classification. Consulting a tax professional familiar with local laws can provide deeper insights and avoid potential pitfalls.

Pass-through taxation offers a streamlined approach for LLCs and other qualifying entities, lowering duplicative tax burdens and allowing agile financial planning. As business dynamics continue to change, having a solid grasp of these mechanics gives owners the confidence to make informed choices regarding growth, investment, and compliance. When you understand the options available and choose the optimal path forward, you can improve your operations while securing greater financial health and resilience.

Comparing Pass-Through to Double Taxation

When considering tax structures, one fundamental distinction is between pass-through taxation and double taxation. Traditional corporations, known as C corporations, face the challenge of double taxation. This means that the corporation itself is taxed on its earnings at the corporate level, and then shareholders are taxed again on any dividends they receive.

Taxation Layers

This is a two-tiered tax system that can significantly impact overall profitability. Conversely, pass-through entities like S corporations, partnerships, and LLCs avoid this dual layer of taxation because their profits flow directly to the owners or shareholders, who then report them on their individual income tax returns. Thus, owners face taxation only once, usually resulting in significant tax savings.

Financial Implications

From a financial perspective, double taxation can erode a company's earnings. For instance, after paying corporate taxes, a C corporation may want to reinvest its remaining profits into growth opportunities. However, when those profits later are distributed as dividends, they become subject to personal income tax for the shareholders. This second layer of taxation lowers the incentives for reinvestment and profit retention, potentially hindering the company's growth trajectory.

In contrast, pass-through entities offer an easier approach where profits can be retained for business development without the additional tax burden, improving their ability to accumulate capital over time. The ease of transferring tax obligations from the entity to the individual helps maintain liquidity, allowing for more strategic financial planning.

The choice of business structure directly affects tax efficiency. Entrepreneurs must weigh their options carefully, keeping in mind that each structure carries its tax implications. An S corporation might be preferable for businesses intending to divide shares among multiple shareholders without facing double taxation. On the flip side, an LLC offers flexibility with fewer restrictions on ownership and management, serving well those who wish to combine the benefits of pass-through taxation with limited liability protection.

Optimal Structure Decisions

When choosing your business structure, consider factors such as the potential number of owners, how complex you want operations to be, and long-term financial goals. For entities with high initial capital needs or plans for public offerings, traditional C corporations may still be advantageous due to their ability to attract investors through stock sales. However, for small businesses prioritizing immediate tax efficiency, pass-through entities typically present a more favorable option.

Case Studies

Let's have a look at the advantages of pass-through taxation. Take, for example, a boutique photography studio that specializes in corporate events and weddings. This LLC generated $180,000 in revenue last year. Through pass-through taxation, this income goes directly to the owner's personal tax return. In this case, the owner is in the 32% tax bracket, but they are still only taxed once, which makes it an advantage.

Similarly, consider a tech startup structured as an S corporation. With several shareholders contributing varying levels of expertise and capital, an S corporation allows for an equitable distribution of profits without the complication of double taxation. Each shareholder is taxed based on their share of the corporation's income, aligning tax responsibilities with ownership interests and facilitating straightforward financial reporting.

Impact on Personal Income Tax

Pass-through taxation has significant implications for LLC owners, especially when it comes to personal income tax levels. This taxation system means that the income of the LLC is not taxed at the business level but instead passes through to the individual members or owners, who then report it on their personal tax returns. This approach simplifies the tax process in several ways and offers unique benefits and responsibilities.

Income Reporting

One of the main aspects of pass-through taxation is the way LLC owners report their income. For single-owner LLCs, income and expenses are detailed using Form 1040 Schedule C. In contrast, multi-member LLCs use a slightly more complex process by distributing Schedule K-1 forms to all members. These forms detail each member's share of the LLC's income, deductions, and credits. Subsequently, this information is reported on the members' individual income tax returns, specifically on Part II of Schedule E, along with other indicated forms.

Potential Tax Savings

Yet another benefit of pass-through taxation is the potential savings from the deductibility of business losses on personal returns. When an LLC incurs a loss, that loss can offset other income on the owner's personal tax return, which could significantly reduce the overall taxable income. This direct connection allows LLC owners to leverage business losses to lower their personal tax liability. When LLC owners understand these tax advantages, they make better financial planning and improve their tax strategy over time.

Self-Employment Taxes

Self-employment taxes also apply to LLCs under pass-through taxation. While LLC owners avoid corporate-level taxes, they must pay self-employment taxes, which cover Social Security and Medicare. These taxes are mandated by federal law and usually amount to roughly 15.3% of net earnings. LLC owners must understand these obligations to avoid penalties and interest charges due to late payments. They also need a strategy that includes making quarterly estimated tax payments to avoid unexpected liabilities at year-end (*About Schedule C (Form 1040)...*, 2024).

Retirement Contributions

Retirement planning is also an advantage LLC owners can benefit from under pass-through taxation. Retirement contributions work with personal financial strategies, creating long-term savings and tax benefits. For example, LLC owners might establish solo 401(k) plans, which allow them to make significant pre-tax contributions. This setup lowers their current taxable income while building a retirement nest egg. You can also use a Simplified Employee Pension (SEP) IRA that offers flexible contribution limits that align with business profits (Murphy, 2024). When LLC owners choose the right retirement options, they make wise investment choices, which in turn improve both current tax savings and future financial security.

Strategic Planning for Income Distribution

Smart income distribution planning under pass-through taxation helps small business owners reduce their tax costs. As you set up an LLC or similar entity, knowing the distinctions between owner distributions and salary payments changes your tax amount. One of the primary benefits of focusing on these differences lies in the potential for optimizing after-tax income.

Distributions vs. Salaries

Owner distributions refer to the profits that are allocated to the members of a pass-through entity. Unlike traditional salary payments, which are subject to payroll taxes, distributions typically aren't taxed at the entity level. This means that owners might only pay personal income tax on these amounts, reducing overall tax liability. On the other hand, salary payments offer the benefit of being deductible as a business expense, providing a reduction in taxable income at the business level. Make sure your profit distribution and salary are based on your financial goals and tax-saving strategy.

Tax Bracket Considerations

When considering how income distribution impacts personal tax brackets, it's crucial to thoroughly examine your current and projected tax situation. Different income amounts can push an individual into higher tax brackets, potentially increasing their tax burden. For instance, receiving a significant salary might elevate your taxable income into a higher bracket, raising the amount of tax owed. However, strategic distributions could be spread over several years to maintain a lower effective tax rate. When you understand how different types of income affect tax brackets, you will keep more of your after-tax income in your pocket.

Timing of Distributions

Planning when to take distributions helps increase tax efficiency across different tax years. You can speed up distributions during years when you expect lower income to keep you in a lower tax bracket. Or, you can push income to future years where you anticipate having deductions or losses, which can also reduce your tax liabilities. Make informed decisions based on anticipated earnings and expenses. Owners should not overlook the importance of planning around significant life events or changes in tax regulations, which may alter the most beneficial time frames for distributions.

Consulting Experts

Given the complexities involved in income distribution strategies, it is highly recommended that you consult experts such as tax advisors or accountants. These professionals can provide tailored advice based on your business structure and financial situation. They bring a wealth of knowledge on the latest tax laws and IRS regulations, making sure that your strategy aligns with legal requirements and maximizes financial outcomes. Engaging with experts can elevate the efficacy of your tax planning, offering peace of mind while enhancing your financial performance.

Final Insights

Let's summarize what we've learned about pass-through taxation and how it can be a game-changer for small business owners. When profits "pass-through" the corporate tax level and land straight on personal tax returns, it simplifies things while cutting down on hefty tax bills. For LLC folks, understanding these ins and outs lets them strategize smartly, lining up their expenses and investments with ease.

When choosing your business structure, you should know which entities get pass-through status. Sole proprietorships, partnerships, LLCs, and S corporations all fit the bill, each with its own quirks but sharing the same benefit of bypassing entity-level taxes. We've learned quite a bit about the different taxes and deductions and how to maximize your profits, so in the following chapter, we will get into how you can actually form and manage your LLC.

Chapter 7: LLC Formation and Management

Forming and managing an LLC is really about taking a few fundamental steps. From picking the perfect name that represents your brand to making sure you check all the legal boxes, starting an LLC involves some important groundwork. But don't worry; once you've laid the foundation, you'll be set up for smooth sailing. It's like building a house—you need a strong base before adding the fancy stuff on top. It's also important to understand what kind of management style fits your business best because the way you run your LLC can shape its future success. Remember, each step helps establish your LLC as a distinct entity that is ready to stand out in the business world.

We're going to get into the essentials of LLC formation and management. We'll talk about naming regulations and explore the paperwork needed to get your LLC officially recognized by the state. We'll also talk about securing an EIN and why that's important for your business's financial health. There's also loads of practical advice on adhering to state-specific requirements, which vary widely across the U.S.

Steps to Forming an LLC

When forming an LLC, one of the first critical steps is choosing a business name. Your business name represents your brand and satisfies legal standards. You need to choose a distinct name that matches your company's values while following state rules by avoiding existing business names and trademarks. This means avoiding names already in use or those that might infringe on existing trademarks. For legal protection, search your state's LLC database or talk to an attorney. Remember, a catchy name can boost your marketing efforts, but it must not come at the cost of legal trouble.

Filing Articles of Organization

Once you have your business name down, the next step is filing the Articles of Organization. This official document legally establishes your LLC with the state. These articles may go by other names, such as Certificate of Formation, depending on where you're setting up your LLC. Regardless of phrasing, the form typically requires important information like the LLC's name, principal location, purpose, and details of the registered agent. It may also ask whether the business will be member-managed or manager-managed (Feldman, 2022). Getting these details right matters since mistakes may cause processing holdups and legal issues.

Obtaining an EIN

Securing an EIN from the IRS is another foundational step. An EIN is like a social security number for your business and offers a multitude of benefits. It's relevant for tax purposes and is required if you plan to hire employees. An EIN can help segregate personal and business finances, which is important for maintaining limited liability protection. You can obtain an EIN easily through the IRS website, a straightforward process that helps you to get bank accounts and apply for business licenses. Having this number is important to establishing your LLC as a separate legal entity in the eyes of federal institutions (Murphy, 2024).

State-Specific Requirements

Navigating state-specific requirements is another area worth attention. States have different mandates concerning LLC formation, including varying fees, documentation, and sometimes even publication requirements. For instance, some states need to publish a notice in local newspapers when forming an LLC. Failure to comply with these can result in fines or delayed processing. Therefore, performing thorough research or consulting legal counsel to understand what applies to your situation is critical. Not only does this keep you compliant, but it also safeguards your LLC's future operations by preempting potential legal issues.

Legal Compliance Essentials

Let's discuss the aspects of maintaining compliance as an LLC that are relevant to your business's longevity and success. Following these rules is far more than basic compliance. You're creating a strong base for future success while safeguarding what you own.

Annual Reporting

One of the main obligations you will encounter as an LLC owner is annual reporting. You must file annual reports with your state to keep your LLC status active. These reports typically include information such as the LLC's address, the names of its members or managers, and sometimes financial summaries. Failing to submit these reports on time can lead to penalties, late fees, and even the administrative dissolution of your LLC. You can set up alerts or assign someone to handle these deadlines, as staying ahead with your annual reporting shows professionalism and commitment to regulatory standards.

Business Licenses and Permits

As an LLC, you'll need various licenses and permits to operate legally, depending on your industry and location. For example, running a restaurant needs health permits, maybe a liquor license, and business registration with the local authorities. A tech startup might need specific IT certifications or electronic retail permissions. These papers confirm your right to do business and shield your company against lawsuits and penalties. It's advisable to research the specific requirements for your industry and consult with governmental agencies or legal experts, so you know there's complete compliance. Regularly reviewing and renewing these licenses and permits is essential to avoid unexpected interruptions to your operations.

Tax Obligations

Understanding and meeting your tax obligations is another relevant aspect of running an LLC. While LLCs benefit from pass-through taxation, they still bear responsibilities like sales taxes, employment taxes, and potentially state-specific taxes. If you have employees, you'll need to manage payroll taxes accurately. If you sell goods, collecting and remitting sales tax is obligatory. To manage these tasks efficiently, consider setting up accounting systems and seeking professional advice from tax accountants. They can help you go through the complexities and changes in tax laws, providing peace of mind and allowing you to focus more on your core business activities. Keeping organized records and staying informed about filing deadlines can help you avoid unnecessary penalties or audits.

Insurance Requirements

Securing appropriate insurance coverage is a proactive step in safeguarding your business assets. Liability insurance is often a must-have, protecting your company from lawsuits or claims resulting from accidents, injuries, or damages. Depending on your industry, you might also require additional insurance types, such as property, professional liability, or workers' compensation insurance. Check your coverage often, particularly during major shifts in how you run your business. This keeps your protection up to date. Partnering with a knowledgeable insurance broker can provide important information about the best options available and customize specifically to your industry's demands. Insurance is something you have to have. Think of it as a shield against business risks.

Management Structure Options

Small business owners have two primary options when deciding how to manage an LLC: member-managed and manager-managed structures. Each comes with different roles, pros, and cons that suit varying business objectives. Understanding these management styles can help you choose the best one for your operational goals.

Member-Managed vs. Manager-Managed

In a member-managed LLC, all members are involved in making business decisions. This structure is ideal if the members wish to actively participate in daily operations and decision-making processes. It's particularly popular among small businesses or family-run companies where the number of members is limited, allowing for efficient communication and decision-making. If you directly interact with customers or provide services yourself, a member-managed structure gives you the flexibility to make immediate decisions without seeking additional approval. This setup tends to be less expensive to operate because it doesn't require hiring outside managers (Prakash, 2020).

A manager-managed LLC is one in which members appoint one or more managers to handle the business's daily affairs. This means not all members engage in daily decision-making, which is great for LLCs with many members or those where some prefer to be passive investors. This structure allows experienced managers to oversee business operations without continual input from all members. Such a setup also appeals to members who lack expertise or interest in overseeing company intricacies. Additionally, having professional managers can improve the company's credibility with banks and other institutions.

Decision-making Processes

Making decisions in your LLC's management structure matters. For example, member-managed LLCs usually adhere to majority-rule voting for routine decisions, while critical changes might demand unanimous consent. Manager-managed LLCs let designated managers make decisions without needing every member's approval. When you establish decision-making procedures, your LLC runs smoothly and keeps its liability protections, showing everyone what they can and can't do and the implications of their choices.

Roles and Responsibilities

Clearly defining roles and responsibilities within an LLC helps prevent conflicts and promotes accountability. In a member-managed LLC, each member might take on specific tasks according to their skills, like managing finances or overseeing sales. In a manager-managed LLC, roles are more formally assigned to include operational managers who execute day-to-day functions while owners focus on broader strategic oversight. Both structures benefit significantly from crafting a detailed operating agreement that outlines these roles and responsibilities. The documents involved are a map, detailing each party's duties and providing clarity to prevent future disputes.

Amendments to Structure

You can change the management structure of an LLC if it helps your business succeed as it gets bigger. You need the option to adapt your structure to changing needs, whether that means transitioning to a manager-managed model as your company expands or modifying decision-making processes to accommodate new members. And so, clear communication among members matters before making management changes. Keep discussions transparent, making sure every member understands why changes are proposed and how they will affect management roles and responsibilities. Updating your operating agreement with these changes keeps legal compliance while matching your business objectives. Often review your LLC's management plan so it fits your business's current needs.

The Role of Operating Agreements

Understanding the importance of an operating agreement for your LLC can't be overstated. Think of it as the backbone of your business entity. It outlines how your LLC will operate, defining things like roles and responsibilities, decision-making processes, and financial dealings between members. Your operating agreement provides legal protection against disputes that can arise among members. When you spell out your business operations and member duties, you reduce misunderstandings and avoid conflicts.

Essential Components

When getting into the essential components of an operating agreement, you'll find several main elements that are important to include. For instance, specifying ownership percentages is critical. This percentage clarifies each member's stake in the company and helps allocate profits and losses appropriately. Another important aspect is establishing voting rights. Clearly defined voting procedures allow everyone to understand how decisions will be made. This method could be by majority or based on ownership percentage. This clarity averts potential disputes about who has the final say in company matters. Including these components can help maintain harmony among LLC members and help the operations go smoothly (*Voting Interest Model–Corporations and Similar Entities*, 2023).

Dispute Resolution Procedures

How you settle disputes among members should be included in your operating agreement. Conflict in business is almost inevitable, but having dispute resolution procedures in place can significantly lower the risks and costs associated with disagreements. You want a plan that addresses everything from small internal conflicts to more significant disagreements over business practices or policy changes. The agreement should specify preferred methods for resolving disputes, such as mediation or arbitration, rather than jumping straight to litigation. Writing clear dispute rules saves time and resources and creates better teamwork within the LLC.

Customization for Business Needs

One size certainly doesn't fit all when it comes to an operating agreement. Customization is important to meet your specific business's unique characteristics and needs. Just as every LLC is different, so too should its operating agreement reflect those differences. You can adjust roles and responsibilities based on the skills and ambitions of your members and change financial strategies for better results. Frequent updates to the agreement keep it matching with changing business goals and legal requirements. Customization allows you to tailor the agreement to support current operations and long-term strategy, offering your LLC a solid framework for success (Karkason, 2024).

While discussing the purpose of an operating agreement, it's helpful to look at its role as a roadmap for running your business. Beyond preventing disputes, it guides day-to-day operations and strategic decisions, giving you a clear blueprint so all members can be aligned. When you set rules on how important decisions are made through unanimous consent or voting, and list individual roles, your agreement helps handle difficult situations your business could face. Having this clearly documented is invaluable, especially when unforeseen challenges arise.

Getting back to essential components, you'll also need to address management structures within the operating agreement. Are you going for a member-managed structure where everyone has a say in the daily operations, or a manager-managed setup where appointed individuals handle the operational side while others take on advisory roles? Defining this helps steer the company's direction and keeps tasks and decisions well-organized. It establishes accountability and delineates who is responsible for what, which is important for operational efficiency (Karkason, 2024).

On the topic of dispute resolution procedures, think of them as safeguards for your business harmony. A well-thought-out conflict resolution section can be used as a buffer that keeps personal disagreements from spilling over into business operations. With mechanisms like mediation outlined, members have a predefined path to follow, which can defuse tensions before they escalate. It's a way of promoting a cooperative culture that can withstand internal friction or external pressures.

Summary and Reflections

Starting an LLC is straightforward when you lay down the proper foundation for your business success. From picking a catchy yet compliant name to securing that all-important EIN, every step is relevant. You've got to tackle various legal tasks, whether filing Articles of Organization or meeting state-specific requirements, making sure you're compliant and well-prepared for smooth operations. A great start is key, but keeping things running smoothly year after year means understanding ongoing obligations like annual reporting and renewing licenses.

Maintaining compliance after your business launch will ensure that your business remains strong and secure. When staying on top of tax obligations and having the right insurance in place, these tasks protect your hard work. Plus, understanding your management structure and crafting a solid operating agreement can help align your team's efforts. With this said, we will get into how you can strategically plan your taxes with your LLC next.

Chapter 8: Strategic Tax Planning for LLCs

Strategic tax planning for LLCs is about crafting thoughtful and effective approaches to manage taxes wisely. Here, we will show you how you can understand seemingly complex tax obligations, which help you stay compliant while allowing you to make savvy financial decisions. Here, we will explain the art of developing tax strategies for your LLC, acknowledging the challenges and opportunities that come with this business structure. As we define the layers of tax regulations, we help small business owners, entrepreneurs, self-employed individuals, and even budding tax consultants understand and manage their taxes.

Furthermore, we will discuss various approaches that can impact how your LLC handles its tax matters. We will also explain important topics such as understanding self-employment tax options, detailing the benefits and considerations of electing S Corporation status, and discussing strategies for adapting tax plans in light of business changes.

Evaluating Self-Employment Tax Options

Self-employment tax is a significant factor for individuals who work for themselves, as it encompasses both Social Security and Medicare taxes. This tax can greatly impact overall earnings since self-employed individuals are responsible for the full amount typically split between employees and employers. With this, learning proper tax management creates substantial savings.

Options to Minimize Self-Employment Tax

One strategy involves structuring your compensation correctly to minimize self-employment tax obligations. For example, electing to organize your business as an S Corporation can be a beneficial option. With this setup, you can classify part of your income as salary and some as distributions. This means you'll only owe self-employment taxes on the salary portion while paying ordinary income tax on the distribution portion (Fontinelle, 2024). However, you have to designate a "reasonable" salary in line with industry standards to avoid triggering IRS red flags.

Tracking Income for Self-Employment Tax

To track income accurately, you have to use dedicated accounting software. These tools give precise records and let you understand your earnings as well as expenses. In turn, this simplifies the tax calculation process. When you track your financial data, you can find areas that offer tax savings. As stated before, regular reviews help you meet IRS requirements and make smart decisions.

Impact of Deductions on Self-Employment Tax

You can reduce taxable income and self-employment tax through business deductions. Common deductible expenses include costs incurred from business vehicles, marketing, charitable donations, and professional fees. Business owners should keep records of all expenditures to take full advantage of these deductions.

Here's how to reduce your self-employment tax. First, consider if the S Corporation election fits your business structure. While it offers potential savings on self-employment taxes by reducing the income subject to these taxes, it's important to weigh the additional start-up and ongoing legal costs against these savings. Some states impose specific requirements or fees on S Corporations, so conducting thorough research or seeking expert advice is advisable (Fontinelle, 2024).

Track your income correctly so you're not caught off-guard at tax time. You can use accounting software to automate tracking processes, reduce errors, and save time.

Knowing the impact of various business deductions helps improve tax efficiency. Say, for instance, regularly itemizing deductions instead of opting for standard deductions can provide substantial tax benefits. However, you must ensure these deductions are well-documented to withstand potential IRS audits.

Planning for Tax-Efficient Growth

Understanding how expansion strategies impact tax obligations is a key part of this process. As businesses grow, their financial responsibilities change, often resulting in increased tax liabilities. This nudge means anticipating possible tax implications before they happen. By doing this, your business can plan ahead and make informed decisions, minimizing unexpected tax burdens and optimizing cash flow.

When expanding operations, whether through opening new locations or increasing workforce size, the resulting revenue boost can push the business into a higher tax bracket. To mitigate this effect, you can create a detailed tax forecast. This planning means projecting future profits and understanding how these projections align with tax laws. Tax forecasting requires an awareness of legislative changes, as tax codes frequently change.

Utilizing Tax Incentives for Growth

Taking advantage of tax credits and incentives can support growth initiatives and result in significant savings. As a business owner, you should actively research available opportunities at the state and federal levels. These incentives might be linked to specific industries, hiring practices, or geographical locations. Sometimes, government programs offer credits for investing in renewable energy or infrastructure in economically distressed areas. You can use these incentives to lower a company's tax bill, freeing up capital for reinvestment into the business.

Besides location-based incentives, hiring practices unlock tax benefits. The Work Opportunity Tax Credit (WOTC) helps businesses. This program gives credits to companies that hire certain target groups, such as veterans or recipients of public assistance. Hiring these individuals earns your business tax credits, which improves your financial position. You should keep track of relevant hiring practices and consult your tax professional about using such programs. Look into government programs that offer grants with tax credits. Grants do not require repayment. Use them to fund projects like research and development activities, employee training programs, or infrastructure upgrades. When requested correctly, these grants improve your bottom line. Remember to stay informed about deadlines and submission requirements for better chances of receiving the grant.

Accurate documentation is essential when applying for tax incentives. Keeping detailed records of expenses and tax incentives demonstrates their value to your business and streamlines the application process. For instance, when claiming tax credits for energy-efficient equipment, having records of the costs readily available will support your claims and simplify any potential tax audit.

Networking with other business owners and industry professionals helps. Having discussions and sharing experiences might show new opportunities for tax incentives. Joining industry-specific associations or online forums helps you learn about the latest programs and get insights on handling complex tax regulations. Working with peers improves your understanding of available resources, shows you best practices, and helps you partner for projects that qualify for multiple incentives. Research the options available to use tax incentives to support growth, increase savings, and reinvestment into key areas of your operation. As you plan your initiatives, consider how tax benefits support your goals.

Investment in Assets and Tax Considerations

Investing in assets such as equipment or real estate can lead to tax deductions for depreciation, which can lower taxable income and support tax-efficient growth. However, strategic planning regarding the timing of asset disposals is essential to maximize these benefits. For instance, aligning asset sales with periods of lower income can minimize capital gains taxes. Also, considering the type of asset is advised; some might qualify for immediate expensing under special tax provisions, providing immediate tax relief and improving cash flow.

Long-Term Growth vs. Immediate Tax Savings

Strategically balancing immediate tax savings with long-term growth objectives is also a significant aspect of effective tax planning for LLCs. You have to understand the trade-offs between short-term tax benefits and potential long-term gains. For example, while deferring income can provide short-term tax relief, it might not always align with a company's long-term strategy if it means missing out on larger future deductions or credits. You must weigh the benefits of current tax savings against the potential future financial landscape of their business.

This balance between immediate tax savings and long-term growth goals can often be challenging. It requires a good understanding of both current tax obligations and future possibilities. Business owners should continually evaluate their strategies, looking for ways to adapt and optimize.

To use these strategies, you need a clear understanding of your business model and financial projections. Keep thorough documentation and accurate records to substantiate claims for deductions, credits, or incentives.

Considerations for S Corporation Election

In the world of LLCs, electing S Corporation status can give you intriguing tax benefits. Acknowledging the benefits and implications of this election is absolutely relevant for entrepreneurs looking to optimize their tax strategies.

Eligibility Requirements for S Corporations

Let's consider the eligibility requirements for electing S Corporation status. Not every LLC qualifies automatically for this designation. For that to happen, strict criteria must be met first. The entity must have no more than 100 shareholders, all of whom must be U.S. citizens or residents, and it must issue only one class of stock. Meeting these conditions may seem straightforward, but overlooking any detail can jeopardize your ability to make this election.

Tax Advantages of S Corporations

The primary motivation for many LLCs considering an S Corporation election is the potential reduction in self-employment taxes. Owners of LLCs taxed as partnerships often must pay self-employment tax on their share of the net business income. However, when an LLC chooses to be treated as an S Corporation, only the wages paid to owner-employees are subject to payroll taxes, including Social Security and Medicare taxes. This distinction lets LLC owners classify only a portion of the income as wages, and so reduce the overall tax liability. It's essential to set reasonable compensation for owner-employees to stay compliant and maximize tax savings without attracting undue attention from the IRS (*Understanding the Tax Consequences of Compensation*, 2022).

Impact on Distribution of Earnings

Another aspect to consider when electing S Corporation status is the profit distribution to shareholders. Unlike LLCs taxed as partnerships, where distributions might be more flexible, S Corporations require careful structuring of profit distribution so tax efficiencies can be effectively achieved. Wisely dividing profits between salary and dividends can have substantial tax implications. The dividend component, not subject to self-employment taxes, gives considerable scope for strategic tax planning. Following these distribution rules improves personal tax results and maintains corporate compliance.

Transitioning from an LLC's default tax classification to an S Corporation is related to accounting changes that need to be included in the evaluation. While the administrative requirements might be less overwhelming compared to forming new entities, existing accounting practices will likely require revisions. For example, payroll systems may need adjustments to accommodate the requirement for setting and paying reasonable salaries. Also, quarterly estimated tax payments may be due, changing how cash flow is managed throughout the fiscal year. So, businesses need to conduct thorough analyses to determine whether these changes are in line with their operational capabilities and growth plans.

Challenges and Considerations

Yet another notable consideration is that not all businesses benefit equally from an S Corporation election. Despite the allure of potential tax savings, the transition could introduce complexities that offset the perceived advantages. Companies should evaluate potential impacts in detail, factoring in both current financial standing and projected growth. In some cases, the flexibility and simplicity offered by an LLC taxed as a partnership outweigh the advantages of S Corporation taxation. Each business's specific circumstances play a pivotal role in deciding if such an election is beneficial.

Business owners must stay informed and aware to ensure their chosen tax structure continues to benefit their business in the long run. This includes understanding the conditions and responsibilities that come with potential tax savings and efficiencies, as well as keeping up with regulatory changes. By remaining vigilant and informed, business owners can make ongoing evaluations of their tax strategies to ensure they continue to serve the business's best interests.

Adapting Strategies With Business Changes

Tax planning for your LLC is a continuous process that must change with your business. As your company continues to grow or experiences significant changes, check your tax strategies to see if they still match your goals and compliance requirements. Because of this, identifying triggers for reevaluating your tax strategy becomes essential. Changes such as expanding into new markets, shifting revenue streams, or modifications in business structure are some key indicators for which a review and possible adaptation of tax strategies are needed.

Flexibility in Tax Planning

Markets fluctuate, and businesses often experience seasonal variations. But if you keep your tax strategies flexible, your LLC can take advantage of these market changes. If you know that certain times of the year bring higher revenue due to increased customer demand, adjusting your expense reporting or investment strategy could help manage taxable income better. Being flexible lets your business find opportunities for tax savings that can boost profitability throughout the year.

Long-Term vs. Short-Term Adaptations

You must know how to balance immediate business needs with long-term financial goals. While short-term tax savings can boost cash flow, it is time-worthy to assess how these decisions fit within the broader scope of your company's future plans. Smart tax planning often means analyzing current operations and planning for growth goals. For instance, investing in technology or equipment usually involves upfront costs, but these investments can reduce taxable income through depreciation over time.

Watch for major business shifts to know when your tax strategies need updates. Any change in business operations—be it launching a new product line, expanding geographically, or altering pricing models—can affect taxes. Keeping an eye on these developments allows your LLC to remain aligned with its strategic objectives and maximizes any available tax benefits. More importantly, understanding these triggers and actively seeking ways to respond can safeguard your business from unnecessary tax burdens and make room for potential savings.

Closing the loop between strategy and execution requires a consistent feedback mechanism. Implementing periodic reviews and incorporating feedback from all levels within the organization will ensure this. Adjustments based on real-time data and insights gathered can reveal new savings opportunities or compliance improvements that previously went unnoticed. When your LLC stays focused on improvement, it better handles both internal changes and external pressures like market volatility or regulatory updates.

When engaging with tax professionals, consider forming partnerships with those who understand your industry and specific business model. An informed advisor who knows the peculiarities of your LLC's sector can recommend more precise strategies. These collaborations give you better solutions over generic advice, culminating in a robust, well-rounded strategic tax plan that seamlessly complements your operational strengths and navigates weaknesses.

Businesses willing to rethink tax strategies on a regular basis can reallocate resources saved from taxes toward R&D or expansion initiatives. This reinvestment promotes continuous advancement and keeps your LLC agile and forward-thinking.

Summary and Reflections

Let's review the developing tax strategies for LLCs that showed you how to keep your tax burden light and efficient. You learned how to structure your compensation as an S Corporation and how this can cut down on those annoying self-employment taxes by categorizing earnings wisely between salary and distributions. We also mentioned the importance of keeping detailed records with accounting software to identify potential tax savings and dodge any unpleasant surprises when Uncle Sam comes knocking.

Looking ahead, remember to stay informed about the new rules or credits for LLCs, as this will help you plan better. In the next chapter, we will examine state-specific tax obligations to expand your knowledge of taxes.

Chapter 9: Navigating State-Specific Tax Obligations

State tax obligations for LLCs differ in each state, and you will need to understand how these requirements fit together. This chapter will guide you through state taxes with ease and clarity, so you know exactly what steps to take next.

This chapter covers state tax obligations for LLCs, giving you what you need to review each state's rules. We will also look into which different states have their own sets of regulations, focusing on areas like registration processes, maintaining compliance, and understanding local tax responsibilities. You'll learn about appointing registered agents, checking business name availability, and surviving bureaucratic delays, all wrapped in simple terms that anyone can grasp.

State-Specific Registration Processes

When setting up an LLC, it's essential to understand that state-specific processes can vary. These differences affect how you register your business; being well-informed about them is key to avoiding potential hurdles.

State Incorporation Practices

Each state has its own set of rules when it comes to incorporation practices. While some states make the process straightforward and quick, others may have more stringent requirements that could complicate your registration. For example, some states may ask for detailed information about your LLC's structure or additional paperwork related to your industry. Understanding your state's requirements saves time, prevents potential issues, and helps avoid expensive registration errors.

Filing Fees and Costs

One aspect to consider is the specific state requirements that can prevent costly oversights. For instance, some states demand that you appoint a registered agent who is available during business hours to receive legal and tax documents. Failure to meet this requirement could lead to missed deadlines and potential fines. To avoid trademark conflicts, you should also verify if your desired business name is available in your state. States like California require you to conduct a name search before applying, which can prevent future legal disputes.

Required Documentation

The processing times for LLC applications also differ from state to state, directly impacting your business timelines. Some states process registrations within a few days, while others might take weeks or even months. In states like New York, bureaucratic delays can extend this period, which can then affect your launch plans. Knowing these timelines helps you plan better and set realistic expectations for your business opening. Check the estimated processing times with the state agency to plan your business activities effectively.

Overall Compliance

Different states may have unique requirements that aren't immediately obvious but are vital for compliance. States like Nevada, for instance, often promote themselves as business-friendly because of their lenient regulations and tax benefits, whereas states like Massachusetts have more complex regulatory environments. Grasping these details will help you work through the system quickly and save you money and time.

Having familiarity with your chosen state's paperwork can guide you through each step with ease. Some states require an operating agreement even if it's not legally mandatory. Drafting this document can define your LLC's operational framework, which is particularly helpful in preventing internal conflicts among members.

Local Tax Obligations

Keep in mind that sometimes cities and counties create additional tax rules in addition to state requirements. Many states mandate income and payroll taxes at the state level, but cities like St. Louis impose an additional earnings tax.

Sales and Use Taxes

Sales tax obligations at the local level also present challenges for LLCs. Depending on where your business operates, you might face varying sales tax rates, which affect pricing strategies and compliance efforts. For example, a small business owner in Denver would need to account for Colorado's state sales tax and Denver's local sales tax. When selling goods, the total cost to customers includes these layered taxes. This requires careful pricing strategies to maintain competitiveness while ensuring compliance with local taxation laws.

Employment Taxes

Local taxes can significantly influence payroll requirements and employee withholdings, impacting human resources decisions. If your LLC has employees in different localities within a single state, varied local tax laws require special attention. In Ohio, for example, municipal income taxes require businesses to withhold specific amounts from employee wages, which can complicate payroll processing and budgeting. This highlights the importance of understanding these differences to avoid withholding errors and to manage HR operations properly.

Licensing and Permits

You will need local business licenses and permits to stay compliant and avoid fines. Different localities may have specific licensing requirements beyond those mandated by state authorities. Failing to adhere to these can lead to expensive fines or even force a business to halt operations. Consider a café owner in Los Angeles who has to secure health permits and local business permits to remain operational. Ignoring these requirements can result in hefty penalties and disrupt daily business activities.

You absolutely need to know your local tax rules to follow all requirements. Entrepreneurs setting up LLCs should conduct detailed research into the tax obligations of each locality they operate in. Researching state-specific fees prevents potential unexpected expenses, allowing business owners to allocate funds efficiently. Some states might offer lower fees to attract businesses, so being aware of these variations can provide advantageous opportunities for minimizing costs.

When you leverage this knowledge about local tax obligations, you will gain advantages over competitors. You can evaluate which local jurisdictions offer competitive advantages through tax incentives or lower regulatory costs.

When LLCs are thoughtful about these regional differences, they can optimize their financial strategies, adapt to pricing fluctuations, and refine their operational processes. You might need to adjust payroll systems for new withholding rules or change sales strategies based on tax rates.

For self-employed individuals, recognizing these local details can debunk common misunderstandings around tax liabilities. Often, solo entrepreneurs neglect to account for all applicable taxes, leading to unwelcome surprises during tax season. When you understand how local taxes fit into your broader financial responsibilities, you can establish more accurate budgeting techniques.

Impact of Business Location on Taxes

Different states impose varying tax rates, which directly affect LLCs' profitability and planning strategies. Some states offer lower income tax rates, attracting businesses seeking to reduce their overall tax burden. Others may impose higher rates, posing potential challenges for companies operating within those jurisdictions. Business owners must carefully evaluate these differences to decide where to establish or expand their LLCs.

Regional Benefits and Incentives

Regional tax incentives further illustrate how geographical location influences LLC tax liabilities. Such incentives include tax credits, grants, or deductions tailored to specific industries or activities. These can be advantageous for new or growing LLCs, as they can significantly reduce tax liabilities and improve financial stability. States like Florida and Texas have historically offered favorable tax environments for tech startups and renewable energy firms, encouraging innovation and expansion in these sectors (*Scalable Business Models for Startups in Renewable Energy...*, 2024). You should explore these regional advantages to strategically position your business and maximize your financial benefits.

Regulations by Industry

Industry-specific taxes are another aspect impacted by geography. In certain locations, particular industries have their own taxation rules that can affect their operations. For example, the petroleum industry in oil-rich states such as Alaska or Texas faces distinct severance taxes on resource extraction. Similarly, states with large tourism sectors might impose special hotel occupancy taxes, directly affecting hospitality LLCs. Knowing about these industry-specific taxes can help you maintain profitability and plan effectively.

Cost of Living Adjustments

The cost of living adjustments in various areas also shapes overall tax liabilities and financial planning for LLCs. Regions with a higher cost of living often command higher wages, which can influence payroll taxes and employee-related expenses. For example, an LLC operating in New

York City may encounter larger payroll tax obligations than a similar business in a mid-sized Midwestern city. These differences require careful financial planning so companies remain competitive and viable in their chosen locations.

While tax incentives can offer some benefits, LLCs must research and document eligibility requirements to avoid pitfalls. Missing documentation can delay registration, so being prepared with the correct paperwork is essential for swift processing. You need to know what specific criteria you must follow to claim each incentive and gather the documentation. This way, you can maximize available incentives without creating compliance issues.

Maintaining Compliance With State Regulations

For small business owners, entrepreneurs, and anyone managing an LLC, it's important to maintain ongoing compliance with state regulations to avoid penalties and leverage potential benefits that may arise from staying informed and proactive.

Regular Updates on State Laws

State tax regulations are not static; they evolve over time due to legislative changes, shifts in economic conditions, and updates in government policies. Failure to comply can lead to non-compliance, which often results in financial penalties and could damage your business reputation.

To prevent such complications, consider setting up a reliable system to stay updated on the latest rules. For instance, you can subscribe to industry newsletters, attend relevant seminars or webinars, or even use software tools designed to track regulatory changes. Keeping your finger on the pulse of legislative developments helps your LLC stay aligned with current requirements and regulations.

Tracking Filing Deadlines

Missing a deadline, even by a day, can result in hefty fines or interest charges. One way to sidestep this risk is to develop a calendar highlighting all critical dates related to your state's tax filings. Using digital reminders or setting up automated alerts can help you never miss an important tax deadline again. Being punctual saves money and keeps your LLC in good standing with state authorities.

Implementing Internal Checks

Also, implementing internal checks through audits and technology is integral to remaining compliant. Regular audits of your financial practices catch discrepancies early. Many modern accounting systems offer automation features that simplify tasks like record-keeping, tax calculations, and report generation. Automation reduces human error, speeds up workflows, and allows you to manage your tax obligations better. In fact, leveraging appropriate software solutions has significantly reduced the administrative burden associated with regulatory compliance, ultimately saving time and lowering business costs (Russell, 2024).

Lastly, using audit trails and digital records makes it easier to assemble documentation should you ever face an inquiry or audit from state authorities.

Concluding Thoughts

Understanding state tax requirements for LLCs is relevant for anyone running or starting a business. From seasoned entrepreneurs to startups or self-employed business owners, knowing these rules is instrumental to simplifying business taxes. We've chatted about various state regulations, from registering your business correctly to keeping tabs on state-specific paperwork and deadlines. Staying updated on these details can save you from unexpected fines and keep your business humming smoothly.

Each state's tax offers different challenges and opportunities. Some states entice with lower taxes or special incentives, while others might have a more complex regulatory environment. With this knowledge, you can make strategic decisions about where to establish your LLC and how to manage your finances. So, when you're choosing a location for your business or planning for growth, you have to understand the tax obligations to keep compliant and prepare your business for the future. The future is exactly what we will be talking about in the last chapter. More specifically, we will be talking about future tax planning and the different benefits it brings to your LLC.

Chapter 10: Conclusion and Future Tax Planning

Strategic tax planning involves reflecting on past experiences to anticipate and prepare for future tax implications. When planning your taxes, you'll connect everything you learned to plan and handle what's ahead. Review your current strategies and see how they work, as this creates a strong foundation for managing upcoming financial hurdles. The art of tax planning doesn't end with compliance; it extends to anticipating changes and adapting effectively. This chapter is not just about closing books but also about looking forward with enhanced clarity and preparedness.

Recap of Key Tax Strategies

Running a small business means understanding that tax strategies matter for financial management. Good planning helps business owners organize their finances and prepare for tax obligations. Set aside time to plan tax expectations so you will avoid last-minute scrambles and stay prepared for tax season. Such foresight allows for better cash flow management, by which businesses can allocate resources more effectively and mitigate stress during peak tax times. This approach can make a difference in managing the day-to-day operations while keeping an eye on the bigger picture.

Utilizing Deductions

Track and short eligible expenses to lower your taxable income dramatically. Common deductible expenses include office supplies, travel costs, advertising fees, and employee training programs, all of which contribute to reducing the overall tax burden. It's essential for business owners to maintain meticulous documentation, such as receipts and invoices, to support these deductions. When you take full advantage of deductions, businesses can improve financial efficiency and redirect savings toward growth initiatives.

Staying Informed

Remaining informed about tax laws is equally important in maintaining compliance and clarity amid complex regulations. Tax laws constantly evolve, and staying updated through reliable channels is critical. At the same time, you have to engage with tax professionals, or subscribing to reputable industry updates can provide valuable insights into legislative changes that may impact a business's tax situation. For instance, provisions of federal tax law set to expire at the end of 2025 will require companies to reassess their strategies to ensure they remain compliant. Professional guidance can help interpret these changes and adapt plans accordingly, helping business owners go through the intricacies of tax regulation effectively and stay on the right side of the law.

Leveraging Technology

As you already know, using modern tools improves tax management. With accounting software, you will simplify tasks like invoices, expense tracking, and bank reconciliations and improve the accuracy of your record-keeping. Advanced software often provides real-time financial insights that allow business owners to make informed decisions and adjust strategies promptly. Cloud-based solutions let you access records from anywhere, keeping data up-to-date and secure. The automation features in many of these systems can save time, reduce human errors, and allow entrepreneurs to concentrate more on growing their business rather than getting bogged down with paperwork.

Planning is necessary for effective tax management. Strategic planning helps predict cash flow requirements and reduces the risk of missing vital deductions. Establishing a thorough plan early on supports long-term business sustainability and assures that tax liabilities are minimized wherever possible. Regularly reviewing financial performance can highlight trends and opportunities for additional deductions or credits.

For those new to tax planning, you can explore different scenarios with professional help to provide you with a different perspective. Understanding the timeline of tax obligations, even if it isn't directly linked to immediate decision-making, gives you foresight that aids in better financial forecasting. Although focusing on the essentials minimizes confusion, being aware of potential shifts in regulations can prepare businesses for varied outcomes. You can include scenario planning in your tax strategy toolkit. This way, you can make adjustments proactively and avoid being caught off guard by sudden changes in the tax landscape.

Building a Dynamic Tax Plan

Creating a flexible tax plan that can adapt to changing circumstances is also part of having a financially successful small business. The dynamic nature of the business environment means that tax obligations can shift due to various factors, such as changes in income, expenses, or legislation. Therefore, having a tax strategy capable of evolving with these shifts is vital.

Assessing Current Financial Status

To start, you must regularly review your financial status using up-to-date statements. This practice helps you stay informed about your current financial situation and allows you to make necessary adjustments for taxation and cash flow management. Regular financial health assessments enable you to identify potential risks or opportunities. This allows your tax plans to remain relevant and effective. It's very much like keeping your finger on the pulse of your business, allowing for timely decisions that could prevent financial mishaps or unnecessary tax liabilities.

Setting Short- and Long-term Goals

Create clear short- and long-term goals to strengthen your tax strategy. Writing down your immediate and future goals creates a plan that directs your financial and tax-related decisions. Short-term goals might focus on managing this year's tax liabilities, while long-term goals could include setting aside funds for future tax payments or investments in growth initiatives. These goals help formulate focused strategies that address your tax requirements and reinforce overall business resilience.

Monitoring Tax Law Changes

Monitoring legal changes and networking with peers gives you critical insights into the ever-evolving landscape of tax compliance. Joining professional associations or attending workshops and seminars can inform you about updates. Networking with other business owners or professionals can reveal how others deal with similar challenges. Sharing experiences and solutions can inspire new strategies for adapting to changes in tax regulations, thereby keeping your business compliant and agile in its response to regulatory demands.

Creating Contingency Plans

You can also develop contingency plans to prepare your business for unforeseen challenges. By anticipating different scenarios—whether they involve unexpected expenses or revenue downturns—you can ensure that your business remains financially healthy regardless of external pressures. Contingency planning in taxation involves setting aside reserves or creating backup plans to handle situations like a sudden increase in tax rates or penalties from non-compliance. Having these plans in place shields your business from disruptions that could otherwise jeopardize your operations or lead to costly audits.

In addition to these broad strategies, some specific approaches can further improve the flexibility of your tax planning. For instance, building a substantial cash reserve acts as a financial cushion, allowing you to cover unexpected tax liabilities or other emergency expenses without derailing your operations. Setting realistic savings goals and automating transfers to a dedicated savings account will enable you to consistently contribute to this fund, securing your cash flow even in challenging times.

Another effective measure is adopting technology to streamline and speed up tax planning processes. You can exploit tools such as accounting software that can automate the tracking of income and expenses, providing real-time insights and lowering manual errors. These technological advancements support more accurate forecasting and optimize resource allocation, which leads to more effective tax planning. So, when you integrate systems that allow for data-driven decision-making, you can respond swiftly to the changing tax landscape, maximizing efficiency and compliance.

It's also good to engage in scenario planning to prepare for variable financial outcomes. By exploring potential scenarios and their impacts on business tax obligations, you will create strategies that work for both best-case and worst-case scenarios. Planning ahead protects your present standing and prepares your business for future uncertainties, making sure that your tax strategies stay strong in different market conditions.

Anticipating Future Tax Law Changes

As tax rules change, you need to stay ahead by predicting and preparing for changes. You can handle potential challenges by using strategic measures that maintain compliance and improve financial outcomes.

Staying Updated

One fundamental way to remain agile amid tax developments is to stay informed of updates from the IRS and local tax authorities. Subscribing to e-newsletters, tax tips, and alerts from these bodies provides timely information about new regulations and obligations. Joining professional associations or networks that focus on tax compliance can also be beneficial. These groups often provide their members with valuable resources, discussions, and webinars that highlight upcoming changes.

Using Scenario Planning

Scenario planning involves analyzing different scenarios that could affect your business and understanding their implications for cash flow, tax liabilities, and operational strategies. For instance, what happens if a certain tax credit is phased out? Or what are the effects of excise tax increases on product pricing? Answering these questions before they become realities enables businesses to adapt quickly. Flexibility is key here, as it allows business owners to mitigate risks and exploit opportunities presented by changing tax environments.

Participating in Educational Opportunities

Educational opportunities are yet another avenue for improving one's tax knowledge. Joining training sessions, seminars, and workshops designed for small business owners and entrepreneurs gives invaluable learning experiences. These events provide practical tips on managing tax obligations, maximizing deductions, and understanding intricate tax codes. They also offer networking opportunities where participants can exchange ideas and learn from each other's experiences.

Success Stories for Inspiration

When small business owners reflect on successful tax planning, it's important to have real-world examples that show the effectiveness of proactive measures and informed decisions. When you examine case studies, testimonials, industry comparisons, and visual growth representations, you can better appreciate the tangible benefits of strategic tax planning.

Case Studies of Small Businesses

Let's begin with some enlightening case studies from small businesses that have effectively leveraged deductions. These stories show how taking advantage of available deductions boosts profitability while simultaneously highlighting the importance of proactive planning. For instance, a local coffee shop owner discovered that diligently tracking expenses related to business travel, office supplies, and utilities could significantly lower their taxable income. This approach resulted in immediate financial relief and improved the overall cash flow, allowing for reinvestment in the business.

Another example is a mobile veterinary practice run by a vet named John. In his first year of business, he strategically maximized deductions to optimize his tax position. Operating from his home, John claimed a $6,000 home office deduction for the dedicated space he used for administrative work and storing all medical supplies. He deducted $12,000 in vehicle expenses for his modified SUV due to meticulous mileage and maintenance records. The SUV was used solely for business purposes, specifically for house calls. He also leveraged Section 179 to immediately deduct $45,000 worth of veterinary equipment, including a portable ultrasound machine, diagnostic tools, and specialized transport containers, rather than having them depreciate over several years. While not a massive difference, John was also able to track other small deductions, from his $3,000 in medical supplies to $25,000 for his veterinary software subscription.

On top of that, he also deducted $8,000 for professional development, including continuing education courses and veterinary conference attendance. He could do all of this because he thoroughly documented every expense, ultimately reducing his total taxable income bill by over $75,000.

Comparative Analyses

Expanding on this idea, comparative analyses across various industries show the need for customized approaches based on unique circumstances. Each industry has different challenges and opportunities influencing its tax strategies. Tech startups might focus on early-stage investments and research credits, while service-oriented businesses concentrate on labor costs and operational expenses. So, when you analyze other companies within the same sector, you can discover common resolutions to shared issues and adopt best practices explicitly suited to your field. This reflection aligns closely with findings from a study that outlines how effective tax planning improves after-tax returns through strategic operating, investing, and financing decisions (Schwab et al., 2021). Different businesses require distinct strategies, making personalized approaches integral for financial success.

Visualizing growth through graphs and charts is another way to showcase how tax strategies link to long-term business development. A graphic illustration of a company's revenue growth paralleling its implementation of smarter tax strategies highlights the direct impact of these decisions. If you see such visual evidence, you are often motivated to map out your success using similar methods. This could be tracking quarterly earnings improvements or monitoring the effects of newly applied deductions.

Entrepreneurs who visualize their financial trajectory are encouraged to anticipate changes in tax laws and economic conditions, creating adaptive strategies that sustain growth.

Final Insights

We have covered the main strategies that can make a massive difference for small businesses, from taking charge with planning to maximizing those deductions. Staying on top of evolving tax laws is about compliance but also a way to keep your business agile and ready for whatever comes next. Let's not forget about leveraging technology and expert advice, both of which play a significant role in streamlining tax management and saving time.

Looking ahead, it's all about preparing for future tax challenges with confidence. You learned about creating a tax plan that fits changes and staying up to date with legal shifts. Remember, it's not just about meeting today's obligations but also setting yourself up for success down the road. So, as you put these insights into practice, you're tackling immediate tax concerns and laying a strong foundation for long-term growth and resilience.

Conclusion

After learning about LLC taxation, take time to think about what this knowledge will help your business with. LLC tax rules directly impact your financial strategy and support your business's growth. When you have strong tax knowledge, you avoid penalties and tap into valuable tax deductions.

Think of it like this: When you're in control of your LLC's tax, you're steering the ship toward smoother waters. Unforeseen penalties and stressful tax situations are drastically reduced when your tax obligations are clear and well-understood. Essentially, smart tax planning helps you create stronger financial outcomes. Just picture the relief of knowing that every form and figure is exactly where it should be—it's truly a game-changer for any small business owner.

It's just as important to grasp the small differences in taxation to maintain precise and well-organized records. Record-keeping might sound like a tedious task best left to accountants, but consider it your personal shield against chaos. Invoices, receipts, payroll summaries—all these documents tell the story of your business's financial health. When handled correctly, they change from burdensome obligations to powerful assets. Say the tax season rolls around, and instead of panicking, you confidently submit your meticulously kept records, knowing you've got everything covered. Plus, if ever there's an audit, you're prepared right out of the gate with a solid foundation of evidence.

This leads us to the next pillar of successful business management—proactive tax planning. Think of this as setting up a guide for your business year-long, not just during tax season. Mapping out potential credits and identifying deductions doesn't just happen when your tax advisor sends you a reminder email in February—you must stay ahead all the time. Planning lets you find opportunities that could save you substantial amounts of money and align your fiscal strategies with the overarching goals of your business.

With a forward-thinking approach, you can anticipate challenges before they become issues and position your company for continued growth and stability. Instead of reacting to changes and stresses, you're actively designing your financial future. This strategy isn't exclusive to seasoned business owners, either. It's a valuable practice for startups and entrepreneurs alike, helping you lay down solid groundwork for future achievements.

Tax professionals are more than just number crunchers; they're your partners in understanding the world of taxes. With their help, you can discover information specific to your business needs. They bring to the table a level of expertise that allows you to capitalize on all possible opportunities while mitigating risks.

Consider the role of a tax consultant similar to having a guide on a long trek through changing landscapes. They know the terrain, can recommend the best paths, and help you avoid traps you wouldn't have seen coming. Often, they can identify overlooked deductions or credits that directly improve your financial strategy, translating into direct benefits for your business's bottom line. Their advice keeps you informed and able to adapt swiftly and effectively to any changes in tax laws or economic conditions.

As you reflect on what we've discussed, think about what implementing these strategies could mean for you and your business. It's about building a resilient, informed, and thriving business entity.

For the business students and aspiring tax consultants reading along: Acknowledging the significance of LLC taxation in the world of small business finance opens an array of opportunities for you, too. The understanding gained here provides strong foundational knowledge to help you in your future professional journeys, whether advising clients or managing your ventures.

In closing, remember that your business's financial health is an evolving narrative that needs continuous learning and adaptation. If you understand the information shared in this book, you're already making strides toward becoming a savvy business leader equipped to tackle any fiscal challenges that come your way. The path of entrepreneurship is fraught with hurdles, but with tools like effective tax management, you're better poised to navigate them skillfully.

So go forth with confidence. Revisit these lessons, consult with experts, keep your records in check, and carefully plan ahead. You're in charge of writing your own success story now—one where your business thrives because you took the time to understand and optimize its most important aspects. Let's continue on this path together, shaping brighter futures for businesses everywhere.

Glossary

Annual Report: A mandatory report done every year to update state authorities on basic business information.

EIN: A unique nine-digit number assigned by the IRS to identify a business for tax purposes.

Form 1065: An annual tax return for multi-member LLCs taxed as partnerships.

Form 8832: A document often used to elect how an LLC will be taxed.

K-1: A tax form that provides members of an LLC with their share of income, credits, and deductions.

Operating Agreement: A document that specifies an ownership structure and business management procedures.

Pass-through Taxation: A tax strategy that allows business profits to pass directly to the owners' personal tax returns without being double taxed.

Schedule C: A tax form that single-member LLCs can use to report business income and expenses.

Tax Year: The annual accounting period for keeping records and reporting income and expenses.

References

About schedule C (form 1040), profit or loss from business (sole proprietorship). (2024, June 18) IRS.gov. https://www.irs.gov/forms-pubs/about-schedule-c-form-1040

Behrani, R. (n.d.). *Expense management for art and culture organizations: Budgeting for creativity*. ITILITE. https://www.itilite.com/in/blog/expense-tracking-software-for-art-and-culture/

Beneficial ownership information. (n.d.). Blockadvisors. https://www.blockadvisors.com/beneficial-ownership-reporting/

Coombes, A. (2023, November 20). *Qualified business income deduction (QBI): What it is, who qualifies*. NerdWallet. https://www.nerdwallet.com/article/taxes/qualified-business-income-deduction

Deducting startup and expansion costs. (2017, September 1). The Tax Adviser. https://www.thetaxadviser.com/issues/2017/sep/deducting-startup-expansion-costs.html

Enright, M. (2021, March 12). *What is an LLC annual report and how to file one for your business.* Wolters Kluwer. https://www.wolterskluwer.com/en/expert-insights/what-is-an-llc-annual-report-and-how-to-file-one-for-your-business

Feldman, S. (2022, March 23). *LLC management structure: Member-management vs. manager-management.* Wolters Kluwer. https://www.wolterskluwer.com/en/expert-insights/llc-management-structure-member-management-vs-manager-management

Fernando, J. (2024, July 29). *What is an LLC? Limited liability company structure and benefits defined.* Investopedia. https://www.investopedia.com/terms/l/llc.asp

Fontinelle, A. (2024, November 27). *16 self-employment tax deductions and benefits.* Investopedia. https://www.investopedia.com/articles/tax/09/self-employed-tax-deductions.asp

Hyseni, R. (2023, September 21). *Self-employed car expenses: A guide for small businesses and sole traders.* Cottons Group. https://www.cottonsgroup.com/resources/blog/self-employed-car-expenses/

Kagan, J. (2024, October 30). *What is double taxation.* Investopedia. https://www.investopedia.com/terms/d/double_taxation.asp

Karkason, D. (2024, March 25). *Member managed vs manager managed.* Transnational Matters. https://www.transnationalmatters.com/member-managed-vs-manager-managed/

LLC filing as a corporation or partnership. (2024, August 22). IRS.gov. https://www.irs.gov/businesses/small-businesses-self-employed/llc-filing-as-a-corporation-or-partnership

Murphy, R. (2024, March 4). *Do sole proprietors and LLCs need EINs?* NerdWallet. https://www.nerdwallet.com/article/small-business/benefits-of-getting-an-ein

NOW CFO ranks on the 2024 Inc. 5000. (n.d.). NOW CFO. https://nowcfo.com/now-cfo-ranks-on-the-2024-inc-5000/

Poli, S. (2023, December 25). *Filling out Form 8832: A simple guide.* Vintti. https://www.vintti.com/blog/how-to-fill-form-8832-entity-classification-election-made-simple

Prakash, P. (2020, October 14). Member-Managed LLC vs. manager-managed LLC. NerdWallet. https://www.nerdwallet.com/article/small-business/member-managed-llc

R&D tax credits and deductions. (2024, January 26). Bloomberg Tax. https://pro.bloombergtax.com/insights/federal-tax/rd-tax-credit-and-deducting-rd-expenditures/

Russell, B. (2024, March 15). *Why transforming data management to meet compliance regulations can help wealth management firms unlock wider business benefits.* IFA Magazine. https://ifamagazine.com/why-transforming-data-management-to-meet-compliance-regulations-can-help-wealth-management-firms-unlock-wider-business-benefits/

Scalable business models for startups in renewable energy: Strategies for using GIS technology to enhance SME scaling. (2024, May 5). *Engineering Science & Technology Journal, 5*(5), 1571–1587. https://doi.org/10.51594/estj.v5i5.1109

Schwab, C. M., Stomberg, B., & Williams, B. (2021, February 7). Effective tax planning. *The Accounting Review, Forthcoming, Kelley School of Business Research Paper No. 2021-23.* https://doi.org/10.2139/ssrn.3781011

Simons, T. (2023, September 8). *S corp vs C corp vs LLC: What's the difference, and which one is better for your business?* Thomson Reuters. https://tax.thomsonreuters.com/blog/s-corp-vs-c-corp-vs-llc-whats-the-difference-and-which-one-is-better-for-your-business/

The Investopedia Team. (2024, September 9). *Schedule K-1 federal tax form: What is it and who is it for?* Investopedia. https://www.investopedia.com/terms/s/schedule-k-1.asp

Thomson Reuters Tax & Accounting. (2023, October 12). *Overview of U.S. taxes on foreign income for individuals.* Thomson Reuters. https://tax.thomsonreuters.com/blog/overview-of-u-s-taxes-on-foreign-income-for-individuals/

Topic no. 653 IRS notices and bills, penalties, and interest charges. (2024, October 21). IRS.gov. https://www.irs.gov/taxtopics/tc653

Tuytel, B. (2024, December 9). *LLC tax deadline 2025: Important due dates for your business.* Bench. https://www.bench.co/blog/tax-tips/llc-tax-filing-deadline

Understanding how long should you keep tax documents. (2024, April 12). Iron Mountain. https://www.ironmountain.com/resources/blogs-and-articles/h/how-long-should-i-keep-tax-documents

Understanding the tax consequences of compensation. (2022, February 19). Wolters Kluwer. https://www.wolterskluwer.com/en/expert-insights/understanding-the-tax-consequences-of-compensation

Voting interest model–corporations and similar entities. (2023, July 31). Viewpoint.pwc.com. https://viewpoint.pwc.com/dt/us/en/pwc/accounting_guides/consolidation_and_eq/consolidation_and_eq_US/chapter_7_voting_int/72_voting_interest_US.html

What is a disregarded entity? (2024, May 31). Wolters Kluwer. https://www.wolterskluwer.com/en/expert-insights/what-is-a-disregarded-entity

www.ingramcontent.com/pod-product-compliance
Lightning Source LLC
Chambersburg PA
CBHW030521210326
41597CB00013B/990